D1498050

The Heraldry Book

Also by Marvin Grosswirth

BEGINNER'S GUIDE TO HOME COMPUTERS

MECHANIX ILLUSTRATED GUIDE TO HOW TO PATENT AND
MARKET YOUR OWN INVENTION

FAT PRIDE

THE ART OF GROWING A BEARD

THE TRUTH ABOUT VASECTOMY (with Dr. Louis J. Rosenfeld)

NOLITE FACERE VICTIMAS

MARVIN GROSSWIRTH

The Heraldry Book

A Guide to Designing Your Own Coat of Arms

DOUBLEDAY & COMPANY, INC.
GARDEN CITY, NEW YORK
1981

FORT WORTH PUBLIC LIBRARY

Library of Congress Cataloging in Publication Data

Grosswirth, Marvin, 1931–
The heraldry book.

Bibliography: p. 207
Includes index.
1. Crests. 2. Heraldry. I. Title.
CR55.G76   929.8'2
ISBN: 0-385-14157-2
Library of Congress Catalog Card Number 78–22321

Copyright © 1981 by Marvin Grosswirth
All Rights Reserved
Printed in the United States of America
First Edition

929.82
G

DEDICATED TO

Milton Grosswirth, because he deserves to have a labor of love dedicated to him; and to Adam M. Grosswirth, because when he eventually inherits my coat of arms, I want him to know what to do with it.

Acknowledgments

Many years ago, I took a job writing reports for a market research company and found myself sharing an office with another writer. Shortly after we introduced ourselves, he mentioned that in addition to his writing he was also a heraldist. For tolerating my totally inept initial response to this revelation (I recall mentioning something about having a coat of arms consisting of a bagel rampant on a field of chopped liver), for igniting the spark of interest, for patiently answering my silly questions, for, in a sense, inspiring this book, and, most of all, for his friendship, I am indebted to the distinguished journalist, Marc Rangel de Algeciras, who could have been a professional heraldist if he had so chosen.

In 1976 I wrote an indignant letter to the Heraldry Society concerning the snobbishness of some heraldists, mentioning in particular one who had assisted me with a magazine article (see Introduction). I received a soothing reply from no less a personage than J. P. Brooke-Little, Richmond Herald, who offered to discuss the matter with me over lunch during his forthcoming visit to New York. I am ever grateful to him for proving that heralds and heraldists are not only un-snobbish people of erudition, but are endowed with enormous amounts of charm and wit as well. "I am very much in favor of Americans designing their own coats of arms if this is what they wish . . ." he wrote to me. In a sense, therefore, he too is an inspiration for this book.

As she has for all my books, Marilyn S. Grosswirth served as a live-in research department, remembering the existence and location of long-forgotten books, snagging clippings from periodicals and catalogues, and driving me to the typewriter when other temptations beckoned.

My editor, Jim Menick, must also receive my gratitude for never losing faith that this book would eventually be finished—although I suspect that at times he wavered.

I have tried to produce a book that is accurate and factual, but I have no doubt that one or two nitpicking fussbudgets will find an error here and there. I must assume all responsibility for such errors; none of the people mentioned above can be held to account for whatever lapses may follow.

MARVIN GROSSWIRTH

New York
June 1980

Contents

Introduction: "Why Bother?"

"Why bother? It all seems so—so *affected!*"

All things considered, the observation struck me as somewhat paradoxical. It was made by a lady who, because of her intelligence, personality, charm, and attractiveness was ideally suited for her profession as a public relations account executive, a role that surely calls for occasional affectedness. Furthermore, the comment was made during lunch at the Four Seasons Restaurant in New York, a restaurant to which some people bring some other people as much for its overall "affect" as for its high-priced cuisine. And finally, she was wearing a handsome signet ring on which was engraved a beautiful coat of arms. It was, in fact, the ring that led to a conversation about this very book and her observation that anyone interested in designing and registering his or her own coat of arms was being "affected."

Instead of answering her directly, I resorted to a device considered characteristic of my forebears: I answered her question with another question. "Why are you wearing that ring?" I asked. Without hesitation, she explained that the ring had considerable significance. It had belonged to an uncle, now dead, who was a particular favorite of hers; it was a memento of someone she loved. The fact that it bore the uncle's coat of arms made it very personal and uniquely his. Obviously, therefore, the ring was also now a family heirloom. And, of course, it was a particularly attractive piece of jewelry.

"Well," I replied—somewhat smugly, I am afraid—"you've just answered your own question."

Perhaps the greatest appeal of an honestly acquired coat of arms is that it belongs uniquely to the person who has it for as long as that person lives. Charles Mackinnon, in his excellent little volume, *The Observer's Book of Heraldry,*[1] says: "There is, I believe, inherent in practically all men a strong and lively sense of individual identity—nothing can satisfy it more than a coat of arms. Many thousands of men must sign themselves John Brown, but only one will have a particular coat of arms." There are, in my view, two basic flaws in that observation: First, it is somewhat sexist (for which Mr. Mackinnon can perhaps be forgiven inasmuch as his book was published in 1966). Second, in the interests of accuracy, that statement probably should read ". . . but only one *should have* a particular coat of arms." Unfortunately, thanks to the heraldry merchants who sell "a coat of arms for your family name," there are no doubt any number of John Browns displaying the same coat of arms. Nevertheless, in principle, I agree with Mr. Mackinnon's point of view.

The purposes of this book are very simple and straightforward. Its primary aim is to enable the reader to design and acquire a coat of arms that is uniquely his or hers. Its second purpose is to introduce readers to the "art" of heraldry. (At the risk of engaging, yet again, in a debate over the definition of "art," I use the term here only because there does not seem to be any other one that is applicable.) Heraldry can be beautiful and even inspiring. Of course, as with any other form of graphic art, it can also be incredibly ugly, especially when it is abused. It is, furthermore, a very modern and lively art form, despite its having been on the scene for some eight centuries. As I hope the chapters that follow will demonstrate, it is not only possible to relate personal heraldry to one's own life; it is desirable to do so. Nevertheless, for those who prefer to dwell in the past, heraldry is a gold mine of historical fact and even, no doubt, some fiction.

I have little hope that this book will accomplish much in diminishing the market for commercially produced and sold heraldry, but if it makes a small dent, I will be satisfied. I have nothing against commercially produced and sold heraldry *per se.* My objection is to the purveying of a coat of arms to go along with a name. As I hope this book demonstrates, that makes as much sense as selling you a picture of a total stranger whose name happens to be the same as yours.

And finally, this book is an attempt to accomplish in print what I have been doing for so many years in conversation—disabusing well-meaning people of the notion that heraldry is "affected," which is, after all, a euphemism for "snobbish."

For many years, heraldry has been maligned because those who display coats of arms are believed to be showing off their ancestry, seemingly suggesting that some royal or noble blood is commingled with the more common stuff coursing through their veins. Unfortunately, heraldry has fallen victim to circumstance. It requires no particularly deep insight to realize that snobbishness is a state of mind. For all the scholars and academicians who are snobbish about their intellectualism, there are as many, particularly among politicians, who are equally snobbish about their anti-intellectualism. For every pompous professor who trails a string of academic initials after his name, there is a successful (i.e., rich) entrepreneur who is ready to brag about the fact that he never finished high school. Thus, if there is a desire or need to be snobbish, any medium will do; ancestry is convenient, and a coat of arms is often an equally convenient piece of evidence of that ancestry.

But it is only that. In the words of a U. S. Appeals Court ruling denying the exclusive right of inheritance of Elvis Presley's name to his ex-wife and others, "titles, offices and reputation are not inheritable. Neither are trust or distrust and friendship or enmity descendible." At least, not under American law.

The fact remains that any idiot or scoundrel can acquire a coat of arms almost as easily as he can obtain a doctorate. The acquisition of a coat of arms, therefore, whether by inheritance or design, is no justification for snobbery. Although there may be some who believe that because you are a better person you are entitled to a coat of arms, there is no one who believes that having a coat of arms makes you a better person.

Still, in all fairness, it must be said that to some extent at least, heraldry has brought the accusation of snobbery on itself. I first wrote about heraldry in 1974; it was an article for a publication that in polite circles is known as a "girlie" magazine. It features photographs of young women with few inhibitions, no clothes to speak of, and abundant good health. Much of the fiction and some of the nonfiction also printed in this publication can best be described as intensifying, if not necessarily improving, the readers' appreciation of the photographs. As for the advertisements, the less said the better. At the time, it seemed to me that such a publication was an ideal market for an article on heraldry because its readers, described as blue-collar workers in the middle-income range, were probably the likeliest targets for the heraldry merchants and, therefore, the likeliest to derive some benefit from an article explaining what they are buying when they purchase "a coat of arms for your family name." As part of my research for the article, I interviewed a gentleman whose name is well known in heraldic circles, particularly in the United States. We spent well over an hour on the telephone, and he gave me considerable amounts of useful information which I was delighted to have because, in the interests of responsible journalism, I wanted to be able to quote an authority.

Although I had informed my interviewee of the name of the publication for which I was writing, I had neglected to acquaint him with its overall style and content. He had, apparently, done some of his own research and within twenty-four hours of our initial conversation, he called me again, this time to plead with me not to mention his name, the organization with which he was affiliated as a heraldist, or his employer. Of course, I complied with his request and as a result, the people who could most benefit from his expertise were, in effect, deprived of it. The fact that there was no connection whatsoever between my article and the gynecological excesses that appeared elsewhere in the publication was immaterial. This heraldist wanted nothing whatever to do with it. Thus can heraldry earn for itself the accusation of snobbishness.

Heraldry is also sometimes regarded as fair game for snobs because of its own "rules." Obviously, then, the most effective way of coping with this problem is to eliminate the rules that are applicable. This I have done with a pleasure bordering on glee.

The first of these rules is that a coat of arms can only be inherited, or granted by some authority, usually an agency of the crown. This book is dedicated to the proposition that anyone can "assume" arms, as long as the arms have not been previously claimed by another.

The second important rule is that arms cannot be granted to or inherited by women, except under certain special circumstances (which are discussed in greater detail later).

For one thing, except for a few countries, there no longer exist arms-granting agencies. There is no official body in the United States that grants arms. It is, therefore, impractical to observe the rule that says arms may only be granted. As for women not being entitled to coats of arms, while this rule has solid foundations in sociology and culture, there is no earthly reason for it to be perpetuated these days except as a grudging concession to hide-bound traditionalists who refuse to listen to reason. I have no intention of granting that concession.

These two rules, and many of the other customs, traditions, and regulations discussed in this book, derive primarily from British heraldry. Heraldic scholars may want to argue about whether, throughout the history of heraldry, the British have been the most rigid and diligent in promulgating these customs, traditions, and regulations. There can be no doubt, however, that in modern times, the English and the Scots stand almost alone in their dedication to strict heraldic observance. It may be assumed, therefore, that most of what is discussed in this book is either founded in British tradition or is (or was) universally accepted throughout most of Europe. Where there are exceptions, they have been noted.

This is not a scholarly work. Its purpose is to provide diversion, pleasure, and an opportunity to acquire a coat of arms. Let it be admitted early on that I make no claims to scholarship; at best, I can be described as a heraldic dilettante, a label which I bear with considerable pleasure. Toward the end of this book you will find a Bibliography offering abundant reference material for anyone interested in probing more deeply into this fascinating and seemingly endless subject.

A word about Notes: There are none in the traditional sense of the word. The superscript numbers that indicate footnotes actually refer to the authors as listed in Notes, page 205, which, in turn, refers to the Bibliography, page 207.

Let us now delve a little into the world of heraldry in the hope that when we emerge, you will have a coat of arms for your very own.

The Heraldry Book

1

What Is a Coat of Arms?

Gules, a helmet in profile crested with a plum [sic] *Argent.*

This blazon (the specifications, in heraldic terms, of a coat of arms) describes a shield on which there is a helmet against a red background. Inasmuch as the color of the helmet is not given, one may assume that it is *steel,* or gray. One might also assume that a white or silver (i.e., *Argent*) fruit sits atop the helmet. Fortunately, the blazon is accompanied by a drawing indicating that the plum is in fact a plume. This coat of arms, according to the "certificate of authenticity" on which it is depicted and described, "has been used in centuries past by a person or family with the Feghoot surname or an onomatological variant thereof and are therefore judged to be associated with this name."

This information was received with some small degree of skepticism by Reginald Bretnor, a man who has made a career of successfully blending whimsy with absurdity. Mr. Bretnor is the creator of one "Ferdinand Feghoot," whose exploits have been published for many years in science-fiction magazines. The adventures of Feghoot are distinguished by the fact that the last line of every story ends with an outrageous pun or spoonerism. (These stories have become so popular that even those not directly attributable to Mr. Bretnor are generally known as *feghoots;* among the more famous are those whose last lines are: "People who live in grass houses should not stow thrones"; "Where are you going, boyfoot bear with teak of

Chan?" etc. You get the idea.) When Mr. Bretnor received a solici-
tation in the mail from a well-known heraldry merchant, he sent in
for a coat of arms for the fictional Mr. Feghoot.

Now, then, if Ferdinand Feghoot is a figment of Mr. Bretnor's
imagination, can it be assumed that the Feghoot coat of arms is a
figment of someone else's imagination—in this case, the artists and
heraldists of the Sanson Institute of Heraldry, once one of the two
largest heraldry purveyors in the country? Not necessarily. There
are, you see, several disclaimers in the certificate of authenticity.
The first is the "onomatological variant," which simply means that
whoever bore the arms "in centuries past" may have spelled the
name differently, and once spelling variations are taken into account—as, indeed, they must be—then all sorts of probabilities and
possibilities must also be taken into account.

The most important disclaimer, however, is given at the very bottom of the certificate, in type considerably smaller than the rest of
the document. It reads: "No genealogical representation intended
or implied." In other words, somebody with the name of Feghoot,
or a name deemed to be similiar to it, bore a coat of arms described
in the certificate, or one similar to it, but Sanson pointed out that
whoever that distant someone may have been, there is no guarantee
that Ferdinand Feghoot is a direct descendant. Under the rules and
customs of traditional heraldry, therefore, even if Ferdinand Feghoot were real, he would not be entitled to display the arms that
Sanson had so graciously attributed to him unless he could prove
direct descent from the individual who originally bore those arms.
It is a nicety that an industry estimated, at its peak, to have been
valued in the millions of dollars has managed to underplay. The
advertisements are always essentially the same: "A coat of arms for
your family name." Not for you or your family—just the name. To
understand how a coat of arms evolves from something once
jealously guarded and protected to a novelty so freely marketed
requires a brief investigation into the colorful, dramatic, and often
bloody history of heraldry.

Most historians agree that heraldry as it is known today was initi-
ated some time during the twelfth century. Strictly speaking, however, its origins probably predate recorded history. As we shall soon
see, one of the primary purposes of heraldic devices was to serve as
a means of recognition during military combat. As such, then, its

use is as old as mankind. Families, tribes, and nations have been gathering under identifying symbols since recorded time. Historians are quick to point out that no one knows where, when, or by whom the first flag or totem was held aloft: a metal standard from what is now Iran, believed to be the oldest flag still in existence, is judged to be about five thousand years old. When the ancient Greeks went into battle, they carried round shields emblazoned with representations of a wide variety of animals as well as other symbols. Similarly, the Roman legions carried standards bearing pictures of animals and birds, but it was not until the year 104 B.C. that the eagle replaced all the others and became the universal emblem of Rome. Before very long, those standards displayed, in addition to the noble bird, honorary wreaths, the names of various dignitaries, and ultimately, portraits of the Roman emperors.

By the time heraldry made its appearance, the nobility were already using seals on various documents and correspondence. Owing to the rampant illiteracy of the Middle Ages, it seemed expedient to use pictures and symbols on those seals, which became a kind of household trademark and seemed also to be a natural source of heraldic designs for those same households. Some heraldists are careful to point out that these early uses of marks, symbols, and pictures are the predecessors, rather than the direct ancestors, of heraldry, while other heraldic authorities, in their zeal and enthusiasm, see heraldry everywhere. A heraldic text published in 1682 in London contains the following fascinating discourse:

> I say, while I lived in Virginia, I saw once a War-dance acted by Natives. The Dancers were painted . . . from forehead to foot . . . and carried little ill-made Shields of Bark also painted . . . at which I exceedingly wondered, and concluded, that Heraldry was engrafted naturally into the sense of the human race. If so, it deserves a greater esteem than nowadays is put upon it . . .[2]

Perhaps the most significant "document" in the prehistory of heraldry is the Bayeux Tapestry, so called because of its residency in the Bayeux Museum in France. Actually, it is not a tapestry at all; it is an enormous work of embroidery, measuring some 230 feet in length by 20 inches wide and depicting the Norman conquest of England. In the eleventh century, William, Duke of Normandy, and his armies invaded England and defeated King Harold at the Battle of Hastings in 1066. The tapestry contains 79 scenes, some of which have inspired considerable scholarly detective work and suppositions.

The tapestry's importance to heraldry is twofold. First, it shows that as late as the eleventh century, heraldry, for all practical purposes, did not exist. The warriors on both sides are similiarly clad and armed, but only the Norman invaders carry shields with anything even vaguely resembling heraldic devices, and these are shown in only a few of the scenes. There are various kinds of creatures, mostly unidentifiable, and several crosses, which may merely have been reinforcements to strengthen the shields. In all, there are fewer than a half-dozen designs visible on the Norman shields. Thus, the Bayeux Tapestry clearly demonstrates that heraldry did not exist in the latter quarter of the eleventh century. But it also shows why heraldry became a military necessity.

The Bayeux Tapestry is a veritable catalogue of the military dress and weaponry of the time, as well as the kinds of ships and architectural styles then in vogue. The combatants are shown wearing cone-shaped helmets, with the face exposed except for the nose, which is protected by a guard extending downward from the top of the helmet. Body protection consisted of chain mail down to the knees. One of the scenes in the tapestry shows William the Conqueror raising his helmet, holding it by the nose shield so that his legions could see that he was still alive. In a wonderful heraldic spoof entitled *Motley Heraldry,* the distinguished British Herald, C. W. Scott-Giles, describes the event in a poem entitled "The Duke's Dilemma," the concluding stanza of which reads:

> Now, had he borne a 'scutcheon famed
> That by some cognizance proclaimed
> Him Duke of Normandy—none other—
> He had been spared a lot of bother.
> But in 1066 AD
> They'd not yet thought of heraldry.[3]

Had the famous battle occurred some hundred years or so later, the Duke would have had considerable difficulty in lifting his helmet. By then, soldiers were clad in heavy, solid armor from head to toe and, so encased, were virtually indistinguishable one from the other. Nevertheless, such distinction was essential.

The European feudal system was somewhat akin to modern tenant farming. A *feudum* was a parcel of land held either by the king or by a noble of high rank who, in turn, leased portions of that land to vassals for purposes of producing enough for the tenants and their families to subsist on, plus a little left over to supply the feudal lords' larders and coffers. In exchange for this beneficence, the vassal was required to pledge—and deliver—his undying loyalty whenever the occasion arose. In the turbulent days of the Middle Ages, the occasion arose frequently. (In all fairness, it must be added that the lord was similarly bound to protect his vassals. It was a partnership that, like quaint, obsolete marriages, lasted until one of the partners died.)

As long as military operations were conducted by relatively small groups of soldiers, there was no particular need for identification. But when a major military effort involving hundreds, even thousands, of soldiers was to be undertaken, the result was a conglomeration of relatively small armies, each of which was loyal to a different lord. A dramatic example was the launching of the Crusades, which was a turning point in the development of both armor and heraldry.

In the year 1095, the Seljuk Turks controlled Jerusalem and had been accused of despoiling the Holy Sepulcher. Pope Urban II, at the Council of Clermont, urged the nobles of Christian Europe to amass their armies and to wrest the Holy Land away from the infidels, in the cause of Christ. Thus began a series of nine military expeditions, beginning in 1096 and ending in 1272 (plus two others known as the Peasants' Crusade [1095–96] and the Children's Crusade [1212]). These expeditions did not succeed in freeing the Holy Land from its Muslim conquerors, but managed to provide adventure and diversion for their participants, many of whom amused themselves by looting, pillaging, and annihilating Jews along the way. One could hardly blame the Crusaders for their exuberance; after all, Urban had promised them that their journey would be counted as full penance.

These ambitious military expeditions required the massing of huge armies, which inevitably resulted in rather heavy casualties. Consequently, the Crusaders began to cover themselves with more metal, especially over the face, so that the soldiers were virtually unrecognizable and indistinguishable. Given the composition of the armies—small groups of men pledged to a lord or noble, who in turn was pledged to a sovereign—it became expedient for the soldiers to be identifiable with respect not only to nationality but also to the particular lords or nobles to whom they owed allegiance. It was also useful to know in what language a soldier could shout a command or a warning to a masked comrade in arms.

The Pope presented the first Crusaders with crosses as symbols of their Christian mission (from which the word *crusade* derives). Various records of the period show that during the twelfth century there were many types of crosses, most of which began as strips of fabric sewn to the knights' shoulders and subsequently appeared in various places on the clothing, the armor, and the shields. In January 1188, French and English sovereigns held a meeting to prepare for the Third Crusade. They decided that the English soldiers would wear white crosses, the French, red crosses, and the Flemish, green crosses. For all practical purposes, heraldry was on its way.

The shield, the foundation of heraldic design to this very day, was a natural medium for identification marks. Every soldier carried one and held it in such a way so that while it provided maximum protection, it also afforded maximum visiblity to anyone looking at the shield bearer. All sorts of shields proliferated during the Middle Ages. There were round ones and long ones, wide ones and narrow ones. The shields used by foot soldiers were different from those carried by mounted soldiers. There were jousting shields; there were shields for use with lances and others for use with maces; some shields were designed to be sunk into the ground to form a kind of barricade. There were ceremonial shields and some shields that were purely decorative. Shields were made of metal, wood, and a tough but lightweight substance called *cuirbouilli,* boiled leather.

The construction of the shields seemed to practically dictate the heraldic devices to be painted on them. Many shields had attached to them struts or crosspieces to provide reinforcement. Some had holes in them for the carrier's fist; these holes were covered by large bosses, called *umbo* (literally, "navel"). On some shields, particularly the earlier ones, hand grips and arm loops made of leather were attached to the backs—as were the reinforcing struts—with nails and screws, many of which came through to the front of the shield. These ends were often decorated with devices, such as rosettes. Because of the reinforcing and stiffening ribs, crosslike designs already existed on many shields and it only required that these be painted in bright and easily distinguishable colors to provide an identifying emblem. Other forms of the reinforcing bands resulted in nothing more complicated than having such bands painted, providing designs consisting of a simple bar, either diagonal, horizontal, or vertical. Of course, some knights, no doubt inspired by their fellows, merely painted such lines or bars on their shields, regardless of whether the shield's construction called for it.

No matter how many colors may be available, a stripe is still after all a stripe; the same is true for a cross. Before long, therefore, in an attempt to avoid duplication, various figures began to appear on shields. Animals were very popular, especially fabulous beasts with qualities deemed to be desirable or worthy of emulation. Creatures known for their courage, tenacity, or fierceness also began showing up: lions, boars, and birds of prey soon proliferated.

As the Crusaders pressed eastward in their holy mission, they discovered that the infidels were not their only enemies; they had to contend with the elements. Wearing a full suit of armor, a man riding in the hot sun could be poached like an egg. Should he be unlucky enough to be caught in the rain, he would find that, much like the Tin Man of Oz, his armored joints would be rusted into immobility. The knights took to wearing capes or mantles to ward off the elements. They also wore surcoats, cloth garments that fitted over the armor and deflected the sun's rays and helped keep the armor dry. Surcoats were an excellent medium for decoration, and the devices bedecking the shields were soon transposed to the surcoats. It is from this custom that the term "coat of arms" derives.

In reviewing the history of heraldry, we are soon confronted with a seeming paradox: as the style of warfare changed, heraldry seemed to flourish. If shields, lances, and suits of armor were on the decline, why should heraldry, ostensibly arising from a military need, begin to prosper? It has been suggested that the answer lies in the fact that the beginnings of heraldry nearly coincide with the beginnings of the Renaissance in Europe and England. As military historian H. W. Koch has pointed out: "The sheer exuberance of spirit and self-confidence inspired by this movement was manifested in a delight of visual decoration which found an obvious outlet on the personal shields of the individual knights. It is perhaps with this spirit rather than with military tactics that the real origin of heraldry should be sought."[4]

This "exuberance and self-confidence" were also manifest in a popular medieval sporting event known as the tournament. Tournaments were mock battles that served a dual purpose. To be sure, they were held for the pleasure and amusement of the blue-blooded spectators who, very much like modern audiences, enjoyed a colorful display of mayhem and violence, but without the technology which now makes it possible to bring sportive bloodletting into every home. But also, tournaments enabled the participants to train for war. It was at the tournaments that chivalry flourished. Chivalry was a code of behavior and morality for knights all over Western Europe. A knight was expected to display a love of adventure; unwavering courage; loyalty to his lady, his sovereign, and his church; protection for the weak; and compassion for the wounded. At the same time, he harbored an unrelenting ferocity toward his enemies. (Even then, chivalry was recognized more as an ideal than a reality.)

Place yourself in the scene for a moment. You are at a tournament, seated in the royal box. Before you a joust is about to take place. From opposite ends of the field, two mounted knights will charge toward each other, each carrying a shield and a lance and each intent on unhorsing the other. Immediately, there is a problem: the combatants are encased in metal from head to toe, and there is no way of discerning who is who. Having anticipated this problem, the knights have conveniently had their shields painted with their identifying symbols, which have also been woven or embroidered into their surcoats. Unfortunately, there are so many coats of arms that you have no way of knowing what coat of arms belongs to what knight. Enter the Herald.

Originally, heralds were somewhat similar in function to the ring announcers at today's boxing matches. They announced the names of the combatants to the assemblage. In order to be able to do so, the heralds had to memorize the various coats of arms and the names of those to whom they belonged. As coat armor (as it is also known) proliferated, the limits of the heralds' memories were reached, and it became necessary for them to compile and maintain rolls of arms. As might be expected, these functions gradually but inexorably raised the herald from a position originally equated with minstrels and court jesters to that of a valued member of the royal household.

The importance of the herald can be seen in the fact that he gave his name to the entire field. Although heraldry itself is generally believed to have begun toward the end of the eleventh and the beginning of the twelfth centuries, the term "herald" first appears in English and in German (*herold*) around the middle of the fourteenth century. Given the direction in which heraldry was going, the emergence of a heraldic authority was inevitable.

The knights were adopting devices for their shields and surcoats willy-nilly. There seemed to be no order or design to the manner in which their imaginations moved. Furthermore, as heraldry became more popular, more and more people were adopting coats of arms, and commoners desirous of posing as gentry obviously had to be controlled. Inevitably, there were duplications which led to arguments, often at most inappropriate times. For example, in 1385, King Richard II of England was amassing an army with which to do battle against the Scots. Lord Scrope of Lancashire, a baron, appeared for the muster, only to discover, to his dismay, that a certain Sir Robert Grosvenor, a mere knight from nearby Cheshire, displayed a coat of arms exactly like his own. This could hardly have come as a surprise to Lord Scrope, inasmuch as the design was a fairly simple one—a diagonal white band across a black shield. However, this was not the first time Scrope had seen his own coat of arms carried by another.

Some years earlier, a Cornish squire named Carminow had crossed paths with Scrope, and Carminow, too, bore the same arms. The squire was able to trace his ancestry and his arms back to the days of King Arthur, and ridiculed Lord Scrope as a Johnny-come-lately whose ancestors had arrived in England in 1066 during the Norman conquest. A committee of knights managed to settle the Scrope-Carminow conflict by allowing both men to bear the same arms, probably because of the great distance between Lancashire and Cornwall, and the unlikelihood, given the vicissitudes of long-distance travel at the time, that their paths would cross again. No doubt respecting Carminow's ancestry, Scrope acceded to the committee's decision, but seeing the same arms on the shield of Grosvenor was more than he could bear. He took the matter before a high court of chivalry. After five years of debate, two volumes of records, and far more expense than has probably been recorded, the case was finally appealed to the king, and Lord Scrope was declared within his rights. He kept his coat of arms, but the legal costs nearly brought his financial ruin. (It is often curious to note how little some things change across the centuries.)

Another hot dispute over a coat of arms arose when the explorer, Sir Francis Drake, summarily assumed the arms of one Sir Bernard Drake, consisting of a silver shield on which was placed a red wyvern, a mythical beast (see Glossary). When Sir Bernard learned of Sir Francis' temerity, he was, according to one report, "so provoked that he gave him a box on the ear . . ."[5] Queen Elizabeth I set matters aright by granting to Sir Francis, who was one of her favorites, a splendid new coat of arms: a black shield with a white wavy band across the middle, and a white (or silver) star above and below the band. The crest (mounted on the helmet above the shield) is described as follows: "Upon the terrestrial globe a ship under sail drawn round the same with golden hawsers by a hand appearing from clouds proper, and in the ship a dragon *Gules* [red], its wings spread, looking toward the hand; motto: *Auxilio Divino.*" Thus, while Sir Bernard retained the exclusive right to his arms, it would appear that Sir Francis came out the winner, at least if one is to judge coats of arms by their splendor.

It seems logical that since it was up to the heralds to keep all of these confusing and conflicting coats of arms sorted out, they should be the ones to promulgate the rules and regulations, which began appearing in the thirteenth century. Having promulgated those rules, it was up to them to see that they were observed at the tournaments.

It became apparent that with the combined resources of his memory and his records, the herald could be valuable on the field of combat as well. He could tell at a glance, for example, who had perished on the battlefield, and then arrange for a decent burial. Similarly, he could help negotiate for the exchange and treatment of prisoners, including the redemption of prominent and valuable notables for ransom. One can well imagine that reliability was an important asset to a herald who, on the battlefield, was readily capable of discerning friend from foe. One can also well imagine the disastrous results of an error in such instances.

It became an accepted practice in medieval warfare that heralds would be unarmed, dressed in distinctive garb, and that they generally would not be taken prisoner. (In countries where heraldic institutions still exist, notably in England, present-day heralds continue to wear surcoats or tabards similar to those worn by their predecessors on the battlefield. Today's heralds have mercifully abandoned chain mail.) Whenever a battle commenced, the herald would observe its progression by taking careful note of the various coats of arms. They were expected to observe and report on whether the soldiers comported themselves appropriately, particularly when one or two seemed reluctant to enter the fray. Once the battle was over, both sides would send their heralds onto the field of combat to decide which side had won the day. The heralds used a simple method of determining that fact: each herald simply counted up the number of dead from his side, and the one with the highest score was considered the loser.

The heralds enjoyed a particularly high degree of privilege and respect. They were accorded free passage over enemy lines, so that they could deliver messages, declarations of war, offers of surrender, or whatever military expediency or challenge seemed appropriate under the particular circumstances.

It was customary for the leader of the enemy forces to reward the herald for bringing news, perhaps to ensure that the herald would exercise the requisite discretion. Upon returning to his own camp, a herald was expected to remain completely silent about what he had observed in the enemy camp; otherwise, he would be regarded as a spy, and treated accordingly.

In keeping with their status, heralds were assured a rather comfortable income. For example, their duties required that they be present at the creation of a new knight. According to custom, the knight, upon being dubbed, presented to the herald all of his nonmilitary possessions, or an equivalent value in silver. Another lucrative custom was one that recognized that because heralds did not participate in battles, neither did they share in the resulting booty; instead, they were presented with a furnished house or its equal value in gold.

Heralds were granted almost complete freedom to travel. There was a practical basis for this privilege: As they traveled, they compiled records (which form the basis for our current knowledge of medieval heraldry). Possibly this propensity for peregrination resulted in the fact that heralds were exempt from taxes; no doubt, it was difficult to determine which territory had the right to tax an itinerant record taker.

The most common method of recording granted or inherited coats of arms was the *roll of arms,* drawn up and maintained by heralds. Being, for the most part, men of high intelligence and good sense, and probably imbued with a somewhat artistic flair, the heralds constructed long scrolls on which the arms were painted in miniature, along with notations readily identifying them. These scrolls are very beautiful, very colorful, and unfortunately, very rare today. Some that are still in existence, as well as copies that were made in the sixteenth and seventeenth centuries, have been reproduced in several books (see Bibliography). If you are planning a trip to London, it is well worth setting aside an hour or two for the College of Arms, where some of these rolls of arms can be seen.

The decline of medieval-style warfare also saw a decline of the herald's role on the field of combat, and with it a major source of his income. Still, his usefulness was not entirely lost. Heraldry, it seemed, was getting out of hand.

As heraldry began to lose its practical military applications and became more and more a system of emblems or marks of distinction, it became more elaborate, more ornate, and more complex. The exigencies of battle called for simplicity of design. As those exigencies diminished, restraint went with them. As alliances—marital and otherwise—were formed, coats of arms were combined, sometimes resulting in shields that resemble something of a heraldic comic strip. Various institutions and entities designed coats of arms to depict significant events in their histories. An example is the coat of arms for the city of Oslo, Norway. They show a man with a halo around his head, a fistful of arrows in his left hand, and a millstone in his right. At the very bottom of the shield is the mostly nude body of a woman. This coat of arms tells the story of St. Hallvard, the city's patron saint. In an attempt to rescue a young woman from her persecutors, Hallvard was killed by arrows and, with a millstone tied around his neck, was thrown into the water.

Elaborate coats of arms also depict fearsome and tragic moments in history. In 1568, John III assumed the throne of Sweden. There was considerable bad feeling between the Swedish King and the Russian Czar, Ivan the Terrible. In 1581, John appointed himself Grand Duke of Finland, and shortly thereafter the Finnish coat of arms was adopted. Its design spoke plainly to anyone familiar with the then-current political situation. The arms show a standing lion in whose upraised right paw is a straight sword. Being trampled below the lion's feet is the curved saber emblematic of the Muscovites. But in 1809, Russia conquered Finland, and the Finnish lion took up residence among the eight coats of arms covering the wings of the Czarist-Russian double-headed eagle.

The simple—and, in some instances, simple-minded—people of the Middle Ages became so enthusiastic about heraldry and armorial bearings that they began to assign coats of arms to various notables who had died long before the Battle of Hastings. (Thus, arms of Jesus Christ appear as early as the middle of the thirteenth century, and those of the Virgin Mary toward the end of the fourteenth century.)

At first, coats of arms had been seen as purely personal devices. Soon, however, they became hereditary and were passed on from the father to the eldest son, in a manner similar to, and closely related to, the way feudal estates and noble titles were passed on. Furthermore, the bearing of heraldic arms became a privilege granted by sovereigns or their agents, the heralds, and was considered a mark of favor or distinction. It is not surprising, therefore, that the right to a particular design became even more jealously guarded, and one of the earliest heraldic traditions to be established was that a coat of arms might be granted only to an individual who could then, upon his death, pass it on to his eldest son. (Under special circumstances, daughters could also inherit coats of arms; this is discussed in Chapter 4.)

With the rapid and dramatic political and economic changes of the eighteenth and nineteenth centuries, there was a general diminution of interest in heraldry. But the Industrial Revolution created a community of *nouveaux riches,* particularly in Great Britain, who desperately wanted to be *armigerous* (i.e., arms bearing). They either did not know or did not care about the existence of heralds and therefore consulted various merchants such as silversmiths and printers and an opportunistic breed calling themselves "unofficial heraldic officers," and purchased stationery, invitations, and table settings adorned with heraldry. The result was the appearance of thousands of so-called "spurious arms" which had either been created at the moment of need or were taken because of a similar family name.

Typical of the Victorian era, the heraldry of the period was often excessively overdone, in bad taste, gross, and unattractive. Some of the excesses that appeared in legitimate arms are a forty-foot reflecting telescope in the arms of Sir John Herschel, and "a silver penny on which is written the Lord's Prayer," as well as a dove holding in its beak the quill pen with which one Tetlow, the bearer of these arms, was supposed to have managed this remarkable "feat of penmanship."

It took the Victorians to embellish what was once a beautifully simple coat of arms and create what appears to be a heraldic parody. The great naval hero, Lord Nelson, inherited from his ancestors a coat of arms consisting of a gold shield on which was mounted a black cross *flory* (see Glossary), and a red band running diagonally from the upper left to the lower right. In honor of his achievements, Lord Nelson's arms were augmented, first with a gold band over the red one, containing three bombs "fired proper." To this was later added, at the top of the shield, "waves of the sea, and issuant therefrom a palm tree between a disabled ship . . . and a ruinous battery . . ." And, finally, a wavy blue band across the middle on which appears the word "Trafalgar" in gold. Mercifully, contemporary heraldry has backed away from such excesses.

Today, the heraldic tradition flourishes most noticeably in the British Isles. The English College of Arms can trace its origins back to the year 1484, when King Richard III granted the heralds a charter establishing them as a body corporate. Heraldic authorities continue to govern the granting of arms, at the pleasure of the Crown, in England, Scotland, Wales, and Northern Ireland; the Irish Republic also has a Chief Herald.

Even in countries where there is no formal heraldic authority, the "art" or "science" (*aficionados* use either term; sometimes both) thrives and prospers. Versions and variations abound: on cigarette packages and beer cans, on wine bottles and college rings, in military insignia and fraternal organization emblems. Not long ago, while trapped in a bus that was stuck in a traffic jam on West

Fifty-seventh Street in New York City, I managed to find some diversion by counting the number of heraldic, near-heraldic, or
pseudo-heraldic devices on the trucks that were somehow able to
move in the next traffic lane. Within five minutes, I had accumulated more than a dozen. Some were laughable, others pitiable, and
one or two quite attractive. Nevertheless, the heraldic influence was
clearly recognizable.

It is interesting, it seems to me, to speculate a little as to why,
after eight hundred years, heraldry has not only not diminished but
is, in fact, thriving. It has already been pointed out that the Renaissance, and the attitudes and atmosphere then prevailing, was at
least in part responsible for the proliferation of heraldry at that
particular span of history. Perhaps the attitudes and atmosphere of
our own times also contribute to an environment well-suited to the
maintenance and growth of heraldry. On the one hand, we live in
an age in which our Social Security numbers have virtually become
universal identifiers for any number of computerized dossiers. It almost seems as though the more technologically efficient we become,
the less we seem to count as individuals. Possibly, the resurgence of
interest in having a coat of arms is really just a means of clinging to
some individuality. If so, I am all for it. Furthermore, sociologists
and other commentators and complainers are fond of telling us that
we are now living in what is referred to as the "me" generation,
characterized by the acquisition of material possessions and ever-
increasing emphasis on personal adornment. If so, heraldry can be
responsive to those desires. Unfortunately, the heraldry merchants
—which one British herald refers to as "arms mongers"—in their
efforts to supply this obviously large market have, in fact, made a
mockery of it.

Although some Americans began assuming coats of arms to
which they had no right shortly after the American Revolution, the
wholesale merchandising of heraldry did not become big business
until the 1950s, when the Sanson Institute of Heraldry, in Boston,
launched a series of magazine and newspaper advertisements offering coats of arms for a long list of family names. Shortly thereafter,
a company called Halbert's, operating out of Bath, Ohio, computerized telephone directory listings and launched a massive direct-
mail campaign which the computer had personalized for the recipient. Some letters pointed out that a coat of arms for the recipient's

name had been recorded "hundreds of years ago." Other letters indicated that fewer than a hundred families had the recipient's name, and that, happily, a coat of arms for that name exists. Because computers do exactly what they are told and have no sense or judgment at all, some people with titles after their names were offered coats of arms for such "names" as Sec, Phg, Agy, etc. Nevertheless, despite these gross and occasionally ludicrous lapses, the business flourished.

The arms mongers used authentic heraldic reference materials, and there is little question that many of the coats of arms sold by them—whether in the form of a certificate for only a few dollars or as an expensive wall plaque or blazer patch—were authentic insofar as they were once granted to persons of those names. Where they were unable to find such a coat of arms, their computers were put to work to devise one which they claimed was based on the history of the name. These were, invariably, of questionable taste. (When I sent my two dollars for a coat of arms for my family name, I was disappointed in the results. I sent the certificate to the editor of the magazine mentioned in the Introduction and he never returned it, so I am unable to accurately describe the coat of arms that was supplied to me. I do remember, however, that splashed over the middle of it was a large letter G. This may be heraldically authentic, but I have never seen a style like it elsewhere and I did not consider it particularly attractive. Of course, I also knew that my father, who arrived in this country at the turn of the century, came from the Warsaw Ghetto and barely had a coat, much less a coat of arms.)

I hasten to emphasize that the activities of Sanson and Halbert's were perfectly legal. Both in their advertisements and their heraldic representations, they pointed out that "no genealogical representation is intended or implied." Whether they were ethical, however, is open to debate. Obviously, most people who are interested in or care about heraldry believe that the tradition of assigning a coat of arms to a name rather than to an individual is improper. No doubt, however, there are probably just as many—indeed, given the amount of business these companies did, probably more—who believe that there is nothing wrong in displaying the arms of another if you like them and enjoy doing so. As far as I am concerned, the whole question is academic: there is no need to even think of displaying someone else's coat of arms when it is relatively simple—and, in my opinion, thoroughly enjoyable—to devise your own. ("Pop" heraldry has lately fallen on hard times; see Chapter 8. There are, however, still several smaller firms peddling "a coat of arms for your family name.")

The extent to which the impersonality of commercially obtained arms can reach was demonstrated in a report in the *Heraldry Gazette,* a publication of the Heraldry Society (a nonofficial British organization with an international membership). Mr. Robert Pichette, then president of the Heraldry Society of Canada, received an offer for a coat of arms from, of all things, Sovereign Seatcover Manufacturing, Limited. Mr. Pichette sent in his three dollars, received a coat of arms and discovered, as the *Heraldry Gazette* reports, "not surprisingly, they were not those which he bore with lawful authority. So he and two others, who had received similar postal offers, brought a test case against the firm peddling the arms . . ." Mr. Pichette, who brought action under a law that prohibits false or deceptive advertising, lost the case on the grounds that the company had done nothing illegal, inasmuch as there are no arms-granting authorities in Canada. What is of interest is the defendants' explanation of how they operated, as reported in the *Heraldry Gazette:*

> The defendants stated that the arms they provided were sold to them by Halbert's Company, Inc., a noted American arms firm. They were able to supply some 33,000 "research" coats. Halbert's also supplied Sovereign with mathematical tables from which they could produce on their computer a further 120,000 to 160,000 "non-research" coats, for names for which the computer could not find arms among the 33,000 "researched" coats. It transpired, in evidence given by Mr. Anderson of Sovereign, that everyone whose name began with the same first four letters would receive an identical coat of arms.[6]

A correspondent in a private letter to me relates the story of how, a few years ago, the city of Omaha, Nebraska, became the target of a huge direct-mail heraldry sales campaign. A local radio station became interested and ordered a coat of arms for the family name "Radio." They received the certificate complete with coat of arms and the information that there were only three families in the

United States with that family name and none at all with the first name that had been supplied—the station's call letters.

So much for a personal coat of arms.

Still, does it not seem reasonable that individuals bearing the same surname, if not related now, must have been related in some distant past? Surely, in the dim, dark days when surnames were first adopted, each family was assigned a name that would distinguish it from any other family; that, after all, was the purpose of surnames. The older the name, and the more prolific the individuals who bear that name, the more widespread the name would eventually become. It would seem that the blood ties, however thinned over the generations, are nevertheless there.

Unfortunately, such reasoning is entirely without foundation. To understand why, it will be useful—and, I hope, diverting—to have a brief look at surnames and how they came to be.

2

The Game of the Name

The estimable Mr. Bretnor, creator of Ferdinand Feghoot, whom we met in Chapter 1, wrote, in the note accompanying the "certificate of authenticity" for the Feghoot coat of arms, that he also obtained such a certificate "for a character of mine, named Papa Schimmelhorn. As Schimmelhorn, literally translated, means 'mouldy horn,' I rather doubt that anyone has ever borne the name." Despite Mr. Bretnor's doubts, the name struck a familiar chord. A cursory check of the Manhattan Telephone Directory revealed no Schimmelhorns, but several Shimmels, both with and without the C. I next checked a German-English dictionary and discovered that while the German word *schimmel* does in fact mean mould or mildew, it also means "white horse." While it is un-likely that any practical person would attach a horn to a white horse, it is nevertheless conceivable that an impractical or ignorant one would do so if he wanted to describe a unicorn. Thus, there could very well have been someone bearing the name Schim-melhorn. There is no doubt, in any case, that a large number of people are Schimmels or Shimmels.

Of such stuff are names made. Lengthy treatises have been writ-ten on the meanings and origins of names; invariably, they break down to a list of names and definitions, most of which are of mini-mal interest after the basic idea has gotten through. Our purpose here in discussing the origins of surnames is to see first how they relate to heraldry and why "a coat of arms for your family name" is a basically fallacious premise and, second, to provide a ground-work for using your own name as a starting point for your own coat of arms. (This will be discussed more fully in Chapter 6.)

The origins and meanings of names have always held a fascina-tion for me. There is nothing more irksome than to ask someone with an interesting name what that name means and to be told: "Oh, it doesn't mean anything. It's just a name." Such a reply sug-gests that the individual's distant ancestor, with the skills and intel-lect of a babbling idiot, put together some syllables of no meaning to come up with a name as time and circumstances demanded. Every surname either has a meaning or is a distortion or variation of a name that has a meaning. The variations and distortions, how-ever, can cause the meaning to be elusive, evasive, and even totally obscured.

I first realized this when I developed an interest in the meaning of my own name. I had grown up with the assumption that I knew what Grosswirth meant. From childhood, I had been told that it was of Germanic origin and meant "great worth." But at some point in my adulthood, it occurred that I had never heard the word *wirth* or any variation of it used in that connection, despite the fact that my parents and other relatives were fluent speakers of Yiddish and used that language in their everyday conversations. (Yiddish is, of course, a Germanic language.) A quick check with German and Yiddish dictionaries shows that in both languages, the word for "worth" is *wert*. Where, then, did "wirth" come from? Again, a quick check with a German dictionary shows that *wirt* means land-lord or innkeeper. Presumably, then, a *gross wirt* was either a large landlord, or the owner of a relatively good-sized hostelry. (Unfor-tunately, none of my relatives can recall even a mention of such an entrepreneur in our family history. This is not surprising; the ap-propriate records were almost nonexistent in the Warsaw Ghetto.) I confess that this revelation did not sit well with every member of my family; after all, "great worth" has an infinitely more virtuous ring to it than "great landlord."

It is, perhaps, inevitable that a device such as surnames would necessarily be subject to some degree of obscurity owing to its an-cient roots. The Bible, for example, contains some of the rudiments of surnames. Some biblical personages are identified by their fathers: Joshua, the son of Nun; Joshua, the son of Josedech; and Laban, the son of Nahor. Others are identified by region or nationality; Jephthah the Gileadite and, of course, Jesus of Nazareth. The apostle Matthew is identified by his occupation—Matthew, the Publican—as is John the Baptist. Indeed, in *Matthew* 14:8, he is referred to simply as "John Baptist," as he might be if he were alive today.

The ancient Romans had a rather precise system of names. A Roman citizen had a name that consisted of three elements. The first was the *praenomen*. This was similar to the first names that we now use. The middle name was a kind of "clan name" which indicated the family or group of which the name's holder was a member. The third part was the *cognomen,* and is similar to the modern surname.

The decline of the Roman Empire generally saw a similar decline in the use of surnames, but by the tenth century, hereditary surnames were appearing in various parts of Europe. (The use of such names, however, covers a very long stretch of history. It was not until 1935, for example, that a law was enacted in Turkey that made the use of family names compulsory.)

While surnames were in general use over a broad area and for a very long time, it was not until the eleventh and twelfth centuries that they became hereditary. The distinguished genealogist, Reverend Charles Wareing Bardsley, in his classical work on English surnames, first published in 1889, wrote:

> By a silent and unpremeditated movement over the whole of the more populated and civilized European societies, nomenclature began to assume a solid lasting basis. It was the result, in fact, of an insensibly growing necessity. Population was on the increase, commerce was spreading, and society was fast becoming corporate. With all this arose difficulties of individualization. It was impossible, without some further distinction, to maintain a current identity. Hence what had been but an occasional and irregular custom became a fixed and general practice—the distinguishing sobriquet, not as I say, of premeditation, but by a silent compact, became part and parcel of a man's property, and passed on with his other possessions to his direct descendants.[7]

Thus, it would appear that surnames and heraldry flourished simultaneously and were both considered valuable property to be inherited.

There are generally four basic sources of surnames: *patronymic, geographical, occupational,* and *descriptive* or *nicknames.* Patronymic names are those that derive from the first name of the bearer's parent, male or female. Geographical names originate from an association with some geographical feature, ranging from an entire country all the way down to a hill, a field, or a stream. Occupational surnames are derived, as the term suggests, from an occupation, office, or title. Descriptive surnames refer to some physical characteristic of the original bearer.

PATRONYMICS

Patronymic surnames can be traced back only to a certain point for their meaning. That is because they are invariably based on first names, and the meanings of many of those first names have passed into oblivion. Furthermore, as with every other kind of name, there have been changes in patronymic surnames over the years.

The most readily identifiable patronymics are those ending in *-son* and variations. Names such as Richardson, Johnson, Swensen, Mendelssohn, etc. are obvious patronymics. In Welsh, the prefix *ap-* means "son of." Usually, patronymic Welsh names are contracted and sometimes the letters are changed. Thus, ap-Evan, son of Evan, becomes Bevan, ap-Richard evolves to Pritchard, ap-Rice becomes Price, etc. The prefix *Fitz-* is the Norman version of the modern French word *fils* and shows up in such English names as Fitzgibbons and Fitzpatrick. The Irish *Mc-* and the Scottish *Mac-* are very well-known prefixes indicating "son of." Some of the more common patronymic prefixes and suffixes in other languages are: *ibn,* Arabic; *tse,* Chinese; *sen,* Danish; *de,* French; *sohn* or *zohn,* German; *poulos* Greek; *ben,* Hebrew; *wicz,* Polish; *ovich,* Russian; *ez, es,* Spanish and Portuguese.

Our ancestors, either too busy or too inattentive to concern themselves with details, would often truncate patronymics. William's son, perhaps tiring of calling himself Williamson, would simply be referred to as Williams. (Note that most of the examples in this chapter are English for the sake of convenience and ease. It should be remembered, however, that in general—and especially in Europe —names followed much the same patterns, taking into account, of course, the vagaries of the various languages.) On occasion, a patronymic surname originated as an occupational name. MacPherson, a venerable Scottish name, means "son of the parson." The English name Parsons probably has a similar derivation.

GEOGRAPHICAL NAMES

As suggested earlier, geographical names apply to towns, counties, and countries, as well as to place references such as brooks, lanes, woods, lakes, trees, hills, mountains, and fields. Place names offer little comfort to those who would like to claim a connection to an armigerous ancestor. For example, people named Barclay or Berkeley—always assuming that the name in that form or one close to it has been in the family since "the old country"—can claim ancestors from any one of three different communities named Berkeley or variations in England: one in Gloucestershire, one in Somerset, and a third in Sussex. People named Read and its variations probably owe their name to two or three English villages. As for anyone named Weston, there are over twenty English communities bearing that name.

When Anglo-Saxon was the language of Britain, it contributed enormously to the role of geographical English surnames. Pitman comes from Anglo-Saxon for a man living in or near a hollow. The name Alcott is Anglo-Saxon for "old cottage" and refers to the individual who lived there. Vance and similar names come from the Anglo-Saxon *Fenn,* a fen or marsh.

A curious chapter in the history of surnames is the origin of certain Jewish names. While they are "geographical" in only the broadest sense, they are nevertheless derived from association with a particular place. It was the custom in medieval and Renaissance Europe to identify houses not by numbers but by signs with pictures —not unlike the pub signs that distinguish English establishments of refreshment today. When the Jews of the Frankfurt Ghetto were commanded to adopt surnames, many of them resorted to their house signs for inspiration. The result is such typically Jewish names as Rothschild, red shield; Nussbaum, nut tree; Einhorn, unicorn; Storch, stork; and many others. Some two hundred Frankfurt

Ghetto house signs are currently known. It will perhaps come as a surprise to those with the German-Jewish names of Helfant, Elefant, Helfand, and its Slavic variations, Gelfand and Gelfant, that while religious education may have been widespread among the Jews of Europe, a certain degree of worldly sophistication was lacking. The house signs show that what they thought was an elephant, was, in fact, a camel.[8]

OCCUPATIONAL SURNAMES

So important are surnames that derive from occupations that the estimable Reverend Bardsley placed them into three subcategories: surnames of office, surnames of occupations in the country, and surnames of occupations in the town. Again, what is true for English names is true for names whose origins are in other languages: The English Knight has its French counterpart in Chevalier and its Flemish in Ridder. Carpenter is equivalent to the French Charpentier, German Zimmermann or Tessler; the English Weaver is the same as the German Weber.

A vast number of common surnames clearly indicate the occupations of an ancestor: Smith (both as a stand-alone name and as a suffix, as in Goldsmith), Farmer, Baker, Butcher, Tanner, Shepherd, Judge, Cook, Fiddler, Draper, Mason, Chamberlain, and scores of others. Virtually all of the variations of the name Stewart are derived from the occupation or office of steward. Perhaps somewhat less obvious are names that relate to occupations no longer in existence. Thus, while the name Archer has a self-evident meaning, it was Fletcher who made Archer's arrows. We can guess with considerable accuracy what the first Glover did, but would probably not recognize that Whittier whitened the leather that Glover used to ply his craft. The first Barkers were either shepherds whose names derived from the French *berchier* or were men engaged in an ancient English occupation known as *barking*, the tanning of leather. Bardsley supplies several lists of tradesmen, the first of which "is a record of the order of the Pageant of the City of York in 1415." It contains a hundred or so occupations, some of whose precise functions would require some delving into history, such as: fullers, mariners, tilers, barbers, plummers, skinners, horners, turners, shermans, glaziers, joiners, cartwrights, mercers, porters, cordwainers, etc. A quick and fairly uncomplicated reference to the dictionary tells us that a "wright" was "a person who constructs something." It is a usage that survives in the modern words "playwright" and "shipwright" and one can readily determine what a Cartwright or a Plowright did for a living. But what was Wainwright? The dictionary defines the term as "a builder and repairer of wagons," presumably, of wains, which are large open farm wagons. (One of the more rewarding benefits of investigating the meaning of names, particularly occupational names, is some little insight into the workaday world of medieval Europe.)

DESCRIPTIVE OR NICKNAMES

If modern sobriquets such as Shorty, Fatty, Curly, Slim, Stretch, Red, Whitey, Chub, Moose, and similar offenses against the persons compelled to bear such names seem, at best, vulgar and tasteless and, at worst, cruel, there is some small consolation in the knowledge that the practice extends very far back into history, at least as far back as the origins of surnames themselves. For every English Little or Short, there is a German Klein and Kurz, or French Petit. For every English Redman, White, or Black, there is a German Roth, Weiss, or Schwartz. For the English Stout there is a German Gross.

Of course, not all nicknames are necessarily derogatory. If, even in the good old days, discretion was the better part of valor, it would seem politic that anyone who would qualify for the name Armstrong should not be provoked with a somewhat less complimentary name. Names such as Poore and Rich probably described the financial status of the bearer, although in all likelihood such nomenclature was often sarcastic. Surely, not everyone named Pope, King, Kaiser, Earl, and Baron held those titles; no doubt, there was something in their manner which suggested that such surnames would be appropriate. It is also apparent that those who were physically unsuited to names like Armstrong or Tallman had to settle for names that, while hardly flattering, were probably accurate, resulting in families named Dolittle, Sly, and Chubb (which, in its original meaning, described the village idiot or someone with an apathetic attitude toward work).

Most of our ancestors probably accepted descriptive surnames with aplomb. In the College of Arms in London, there is a grant of arms, dated 1597 to Charles Hewett. In addition to the coat of arms, the grant contains a painting of the Garter Principal King of Arms, also known as William DeThick. Perhaps by the late sixteenth century the name was already inherited, but one look at the picture clearly indicates that it was nevertheless appropriate.

Many of our ancestors assumed—or were given—the names of animals, either because they exhibited personality traits that were similar to those animals or because they bore a physical resemblance to them. Thus, the English Hawkes, Spanish Halcons, Italian Falcos, and German Falkes either were considered to be strong, swift, and predatory, or were distinguished by hawklike noses. Similarly, the various Lyons, Bears, Wolfs, Foxes, and all the other bestial names may be considered nicknames. Let us think kindly of our ancestors and assume that the names originally referred to strength of character rather than physical appearance. (It should, perhaps, be noted that in some few instances, where seals or heraldic devices existed prior to the assumption of surnames, an animal-like name was chosen to coincide with the seal or device.)

Yet another form of nickname is the diminutive. The English suffix *-kin* is an example: Wilkins means Little Will. The French equivalent is *-en* or *-on;* the German equivalent is *-chen*. Frequently, such names also appear as patronymics. Thus, Wilkinson would be the son of Little Will.

Sometimes it is more stimulating to leave the origin of a name open to conjecture. Although I came across the English name Smallpiece some years ago, I have not yet found a scholarly explanation of its meaning. I must confess that I have not looked very hard; I prefer to speculate on how the name could have originated. Perhaps the first Smallpiece was a man of diminutive stature. On the other hand, he may have been a miser. Or the name could have referred to the property on which he lived. And finally, given the frankness bordering on vulgarity to which the simple folk of the Middle Ages were often given, there is yet another possible meaning to the name which, if applicable, must have proven a source of considerable embarrassment to its original owner. Perhaps, after all, it would be an act of kindness to abandon further conjecture about this name.

A casual interest in the meanings of names can prove pleasantly rewarding. In my small son's pre-kindergarten class, there is an enchanting little girl whose surname is Krauskopf. I could not resist the temptation to look up its meaning. Its origin is obviously German and a minimal knowledge of that language already reveals half of the meaning: *kopf* is the German word for "head." It then occurred to me that "Krause" and its variations are fairly common surnames. It only took a minute or two to look up the word in a German dictionary and discover that *krause* means "crispy, curly." Clearly, the original Krauses and Krauskopfs must have had curly hair—or had been bald and were the victims of sarcasm. In any event, Krauskopf was apparently a nickname. Imagine my delight, a few weeks later, when I happened to meet the little girl's father and noticed that his head was covered with tiny, tight ringlets. The first Krauskopf in his line must have had some very strong genes indeed (although they are not apparent in his daughter).

Although it is possible to place a name within one of these four broad categories, it is not always possible to determine the original form of the name in order to accomplish such placement. While the name Biddle, for example, is not terribly far from the original Beadle, it is different enough to discourage a less than diligent searcher. Bardsley points out that names like Batt, Bates, Batty, Bartle, Bartlett, Batcock, Batkin, Tolly, and Tholly, are all pet versions or nicknames of Bartholomew. In *A Dictionary of Jewish Names and Their History,* Rabbi Benzion C. Kaganoff discusses such difficulties, using as an example the family name Balaban. In parts of Russia, the name means "falcon," and could have been derived from a house sign, a nickname, or an occupation. In the Ukraine, the name means "apple fritter," and could have been assigned to someone famous for this dish. A Bulgarian Balaban could have been "great."[9]

Names sometimes change in transition, causing further confusion. Mr. Daniel E. Button, friend, colleague, and as editor of *Science Digest* magazine, a frequent employer, traces his ancestry, by direct descent through thirteen generations, to Sir Thomas Button who, in the early 1600s, explored Hudson Bay. Sir Thomas' descendants settled in Massachusetts in the seventeenth century. One could readily assume that a couple of hundred years earlier, someone in the family was either in the button business or was excruciatingly cute. The assumption would be incorrect; the name is in fact an Anglicized corruption of the French Bethune. Possibly, Dan Button is distantly related to the Beatons, who were also originally French Bethunes.

Names, it would appear, were changed with almost reckless abandon. There were, of course, those who wished to change their identity. (I well remember the story of a maternal uncle who changed his name to avoid compulsory service in the army of the Czar. Unfortunately, he passed on many years ago, so it will continue to remain one of the unsolved mysteries of my life as to why, if he had to abandon the name Katzoff, he chose, in its place, Shapiro.) Others change their names to simplify pronunciation, either because of immigration or because of the free-wheeling spelling that existed in the days of Chaucer and Shakespeare. There are today thousands of American descendants of immigrants whose names would have been different had the immigration officers at the turn of the century been somewhat more literate in the various foreign languages that were spoken by the teeming millions who arrived on our shores. But even before then, immigrants frequently changed their names to "nationalize" them in their new country. Often, it was a simple matter of translation: The German Koenig and Kaiser easily became King and Caesar. During the First and Second World Wars, British residents with German-sounding names found themselves being harassed by their countrymen, and many of them decided to Anglicize their surnames. My wife's British relatives changed their name from Apfelbaum ("apple tree") to Appleby.

It should be obvious by now, because of the way names originate and evolve, that the concept of "a coat of arms for your family name" is at best ridiculous and at worst specious. "Surnames, you must remember," writes Bardsley, "are the simple result of necessity when population, hitherto isolated and small, became so increased as to necessitate further particularity than the merely personal one could supply."[10] To a great extent, the same can be said for coats of arms; the two were inexorably connected. Originally, a youth intent on becoming a knight did so not through his father but by means of a sponsor. Thus, it was the accomplishments of the individual rather than his heritage that qualified him for knighthood and the right to bear arms (in both senses). As the feudal lands became inheritable, so did the coats of arms and the pertinent surnames. Just as one could not assume another man's name, he could not assume another's arms. In *A Distant Mirror: The Calamitous 14th Century,* Barbara Tuchman writes:

> . . . The heraldic coat-of-arms—outward sign of ancestry signifying the right to bear arms, which, once granted to a family, could be worn by no other—came to be an object of almost occult worship. At tournaments its display was required as evidence of noble ancestry; at some tournaments, four were required. As penetration by outsiders increased, so did snobbery until the day in the mid-fifteenth century when a knight rode into the lists followed by a parade of pennants bearing no less than thirty-two coats of arms.

Let us now examine a bit more closely this precious possession, which, despite its exclusivity, you can and should have for your very own.

3

Unbuttoning a Coat of Arms

Any activity or interest which has been ongoing with no inter-
ruption for some eight hundred years is bound to accumulate a set
of rules, strictures, and complexities. It is easy for anyone with only
a passing curiosity or interest in heraldry to be readily discouraged
by the rules that govern its practice. And yet, to do so would be a
shame because, for all their intricacies, the rules of heraldry provide
wide margins for creativity and imagination. For someone who is
considering the possibility of designing and registering his or her
own coat of arms, it is pointless to delve into the more esoteric
practices of devout heraldists and, therefore, we shall not do so
here. The rules we shall be considering are, first of all, basic and,
second, relatively simple. Furthermore, because the United States
has no heraldic authority any and all of these rules may be broken
at will. Anyone in this country is completely free to flout tradition
or breach good taste.

As far as anyone can tell, the first heraldic treatise was an Anglo-
Norman work entitled *De Heraudie,* which appears to have been
written some time around the middle of the fourteenth century.
Perhaps of greater interest, however, was the *De Insigniis et Armis,*
written a few years later by Bartolo de Isasso Ferrato, an Italian
lawyer, judge, and envoy of Emperor Charles IV. Bartolo's legal
background shows up in his treatise, covering such matters as trademark protection, the prohibition of one notary adopting the seal of

another, the placement and arrangement of the various charges (i.e., designs) in the arms, the significance of some of the colors, and how arms should be painted on shields, clothing, and furniture. "The *De Insigniis et Armis* had immediate influence, not only because its author had an international reputation as a tourist but also because it is a very sound treatise which met the need," writes English Herald Rodney Dennys.[11] Mr. Dennys lists and describes thirty-four treatises on heraldry, all produced during the period from approximately 1300 to 1500, and readily acknowledges that the list is incomplete. The number of heraldic works produced since then must be staggering.

It would be both foolish and futile, therefore, to attempt to synthesize all of the extant verbiage into this chapter on what constitutes coats of arms. Instead, let us consider only what we need to know to produce a coat of arms of our very own.

Beginning almost immediately, you will be confronted with terminology most of which will sound only vaguely familiar at best. Many of these terms will be used throughout the rest of the book. Do not be intimidated by them; they are all repeated and defined in the Glossary beginning on page 127.

THE ACHIEVEMENT

Every coat of arms consists at least of a shield. That is a simple enough concept, except that it immediately becomes a little complicated. According to heraldic tradition, women, if they are entitled to display arms at all, do so on a diamond shape called a *lozenge*. Presumably, this stems from the archaic notion that women are not warlike and would be unlikely ever to have use of a shield. It is a nicety that can be ignored by Americans assuming arms or, for that matter, can be adopted by men and women alike who prefer to avoid the military implications of a shield. Nevertheless, the shield is the basis for every coat of arms. Everything that follows is more or less optional.

In almost every case, the shield is surmounted by a *helmet* or, as it is frequently referred to in heraldry, a *helm*. Flowing down and out from the helmet, and behind and around the shield, is the *mantle*, which, as the word implies, is a cloak or robe but which had become so stylized over the years as to be virtually unidentifiable as such. The mantle is usually held onto the helmet by a *torse,* a kind of twisted rope. Over the torse and affixed to the helmet is the *crest,* a device that often, but not always, repeats or refers to the design on the shield.

The *motto* usually appears on a ribbonlike device under the shield. (In some countries it is above the crest.)

Many coats of arms show the shield being held up by two figures. These are called *supporters;* the ground on which those supporters stand is called the *compartment.*

The entire coat of arms, regardless of its complexity and number of elements, is always referred to as an *achievement* (see Figure 1).

FIG. 1. **A Complete Heraldic Achievement.** Arms of the Spectacle Makers' Company of London.

The term *achievement* is not precisely synonymous with *coat of arms,* because if the latter is used in connection with a fairly complicated achievement, it can be mistaken to mean only the shield.

There is a popular romantic notion as to how the arrangement of a heraldic achievement came about. According to legend, the typical brave knight returned to the castle after a hard day's fighting and hung his helmet on the wall. The mantle dangling from the helmet was torn and tattered, as befits the raiment of a warrior locked in the heat of battle. He then hung his shield directly below the helmet and *voila!* the heraldic achievement was born. Mr. J. P. Brooke-Little, England's Richmond Herald of Arms, and one of the world's most eminent heraldic scholars, is a man of too gentle a nature to negate that legend outright, but it is clear that he tends not to support it. "Following the fashion for scalloping the edges of garments," he writes, "the mantling was frequently depicted with scalloped or jagged edges, and in this treatment fanciful writers have seen the cuts and rents which it would have received in battle."[12] Thus, the story of how the traditional coat of arms came about may be "fanciful." It is, nevertheless, a charming one and I intend to give it full circulation—perhaps with the requisite disclaimer.

Let us now go back to the beginning and discuss each of the elements of the coat of arms individually.

THE SHIELD

Throughout human history, and particularly during the earliest days of civilization, the shield has played a significant role not only in battle but as a symbol. As we have seen, it was a practical matter to depict a knight's "trademark" on his shield. But it was symbolic, too. By the time heraldry began to flourish, the shield was already known as an important symbolic and ceremonial artifact. Tacitus, the great—possibly the greatest—Roman historian, in his work *Germania,* written about A.D. 100, described the importance of the shield to the ancient German tribes. To lose one's shield in battle was to demonstrate that one was a coward, a trait punishable by ostracism from all ceremonies. The transition from puberty to manhood was symbolized by presenting a youth with a shield. "When the Franks elected a king, they sat him on a shield and raised him

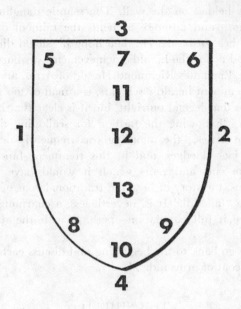

FIG. 2. **Sections of the Shield. 1:** Dexter Side. **2:** Sinister Side. **3:** Chief. **4:** Base. **5:** Dexter Chief. **6:** Sinister Chief. **7:** Middle Chief. **8:** Dexter Base. **9:** Sinister Base. **10:** Middle Base. **11:** Honor Point. **12:** Fess Point. **13:** Navel or Nombril Point.

FIG. 3. **Parting the Field**

1. Per Fess

2. Per Pale

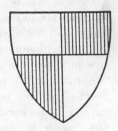

3. Quarterly
(Per Cross)

4. Per Bend

5. Per Bend
Sinister

6. Per Chevron

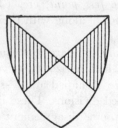

7. Per Saltire

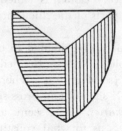

8. Per Pall

high in the air. The spectators indicated their approval by beating on their shields."[13]

Even as heraldry began to emerge, shields of varying shapes and designs were in use. Some heraldic artists have devised some rather ornate and not always attractive shields. An accomplished heraldist can often identify the country of origin of a coat of arms by the style in which it is designed, beginning with the kind of shield used. Nevertheless, the most common form of shield is the so called "heater" shield, because it looks something like the sole of a flatiron. Some heraldists no doubt would have preferred some other form, particularly as coats of arms become increasingly complicated and the crowding of a multitude of designs into the heater-shield outline becomes not only ugly but nearly impossible. But heraldry is traditional if nothing else, and the heater-shield shape remains supreme.

The sides of the shield are referred to as *dexter* and *sinister*, which mean right and left, respectively. Considerable confusion arises from these terms, but once understood, they are fairly simple to remember. The confusion derives from the fact that as you look at a shield the dexter side is, in fact, on your left, and the sinister side is on your right. The explanation is simple: The terms apply not to the shield as seen by a viewer, but as seen by whoever is holding it. To the knight, the dexter side is, in fact, at his right. As you stand in front of him, that side will be on your left. The reverse, of course, is true for the sinister side.

The entire surface of the shield is referred to as the *field*. Each section of the shield has a name: the top of the shield is called the *chief*, the very center is called the *fess point,* etc. (The various points and parts of the shield are shown, along with their names, in Figure 2.)

The field can be divided in certain standard and classical ways. For example, it can be divided in half horizontally, vertically, or diagonally (see Figure 3). There are Y-shaped and V-shaped divisions, and X-shaped and cross-shaped divisions. These divisions are called *ordinaries*. There seems to be some disagreement among heraldry writers as to what constitutes the entire body of ordinaries, but there is general agreement that the basic ordinaries include *fess, pale, bend, bend sinister, chevron, pall, saltire,* and *cross* (or *quarterly*). These are illustrated in Figure 4.

FIG. 4. **Ordinaries**

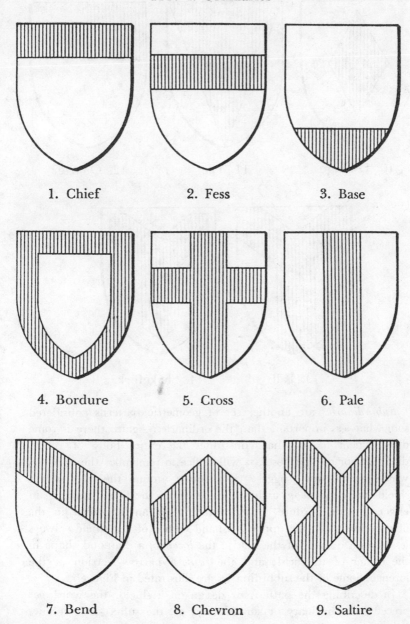

1. Chief   2. Fess   3. Base

4. Bordure   5. Cross   6. Pale

7. Bend   8. Chevron   9. Saltire

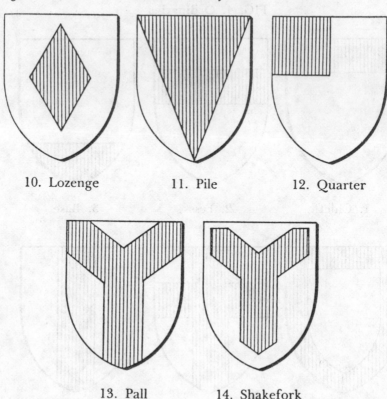

10. Lozenge   11. Pile   12. Quarter

13. Pall   14. Shakefork

Subordinaries are another set of geometric patterns considered somewhat less important than the ordinaries. Again, there is some disagreement as to what constitutes the entire body of subordinaries. For our purposes, it will suffice to remember the *bordure,* which, as the word suggests, is a border around the edge of the shield; the *escutcheon,* a shield shape within the field (creating, in effect, a wide bordure); the *canton,* a rectangle placed in the dexter chief (i.e., the upper left-hand corner of the shield, always less than a quarter of the field); the *lozenge,* a diamond shape in the center of the field; and the *fusil,* a narrow version of the lozenge. Some of the subordinaries are illustrated in Figure 5.

In describing the pattern or design on a shield, the word *per* precedes the ordinary or subordinary; or, the suffix *-wise* follows

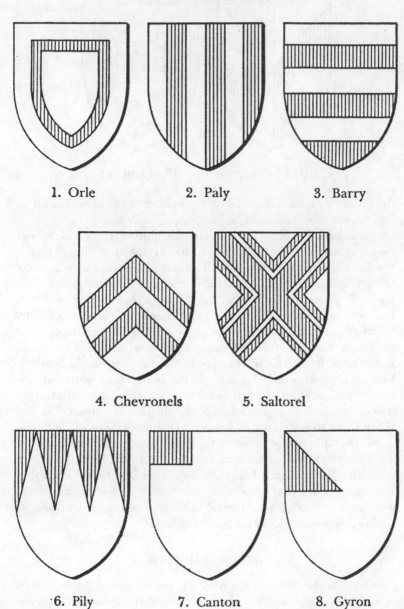

FIG. 5. **Subordinaries**

1. Orle
2. Paly
3. Barry
4. Chevronels
5. Saltorel
6. Pily
7. Canton
8. Gyron

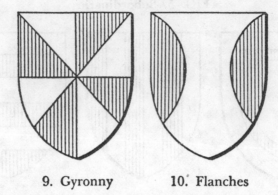

9. Gyronny   10. Flanches

the ordinary or subordinary. For example, if a shield is divided in half horizontally, it is described as *per fess* or *fesswise*.

A number of colorful and descriptive phrases have entered our everyday language from heraldry. One of the more interesting is the *bar sinister*, which is defined in some dictionaries as a heraldic term denoting bastardy and, as a second definition, anything hinting at illegitimacy. What is so fascinating about this expression is the fact that heraldically at least, a bar sinister is an impossibility. "Sinister" indicates that the bar extends from the sinister chief to the dexter base (i.e., from the upper right-hand corner of the shield to the lower left). This is an impossibility, inasmuch as in heraldry, bars are always horizontal. No doubt the term arose from *baton sinister*, a narrow band which is *couped*, or cut off at the ends so that it does not quite reach the edges of the shield. "Bar sinister" is certainly easier to say, and the non-heraldic connotations of those two words no doubt helped enhance the term's usage and popularity. In any case, the baton sinister was used to denote the illegitimate sons of royalty. To understand why one would wish to have such a designation on one's coat of arms, it is necessary to realize that in the good old medieval days, all royal children, even those born out of wedlock, were considered something special.

LINES OF PARTITION

Whenever the division of a field is given or one of the ordinaries or subordinaries stated, the assumption is that the border lines are straight. In other words, a *fess* is a bar straight across the middle of the shield occupying about one third of the area. However, the lines need not necessarily be straight. If, for example, the designer of the coat of arms wanted the fess to have a scalloped border, he would describe it as a *fess invected*. If he wanted a somewhat nautical look, he could describe it as *undy*. The various generally accepted lines of partition are shown in Figure 6. There are some others, but they are rarely used and somewhat complicated and busy-looking.

OTHER DIVISIONS OF THE FIELD

Despite the initial confusion that these new terms present to the novice, the language of heraldry is actually very simple. With very few words, it is possible to describe somewhat more complicated divisions of the shield. Thus, if a *bend* is a single wide stripe from dexter chief to sinister base, *bendy* describes three stripes going in the same direction. If *per pale* means a vertical division of the shield in half, *paly* means three vertical stripes.

We shall return to the shield shortly to discuss colors and various objects to be placed on it. But first, let us examine a little more closely the other elements of the achievement.

HELMET

Helmets were available in an enormous variety of styles and shapes. These were dictated not only by fashion and personal preference but by practical uses. Experience proved that some knights preferred one type of helmet over another in battle. Unfortunately, for some who made that discovery, it was too late to do anything about it. Still, the survivors effected many design changes. Helmets that were used in tournaments and for ceremonial purposes often differed from those used in battle. They could be lighter in weight, or even heavier, if the wearer chose to exhibit a particularly ornate headpiece.

Participation in tournaments was essential to both the development and the reputation of the knight. Although rules and customs varied from country to country, in general a knight had to prove his genealogy, his bravery, and his chivalry, particularly in his behavior and attitude toward women. In Germany, a tournament

FIG. 6. **Lines of Partition**

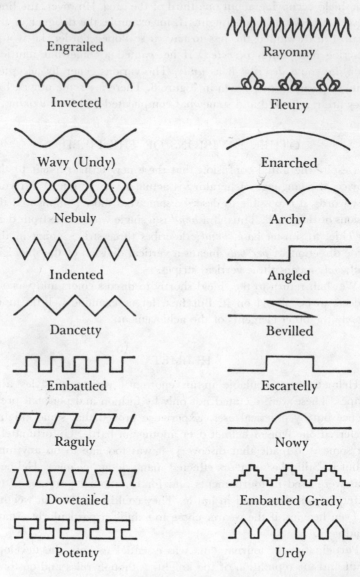

Engrailed	Rayonny
Invected	Fleury
Wavy (Undy)	Enarched
Nebuly	Archy
Indented	Angled
Dancetty	Bevilled
Embattled	Escartelly
Raguly	Nowy
Dovetailed	Embattled Grady
Potenty	Urdy

Crested

candidate had to descend from a line of tournament participants. "And by no means every candidate passed the test," writes German heraldist Gottfried Neubecker. "If the herald rejected him, a pursuivant [assistant herald] literally threw out his helmet."[14]

In British heraldry there are rules concerning types of helmets and their positions in the achievement. The British Sovereign, for example, has a barred helmet of gold that is shown facing frontward. So do "Princes of the Blood Royal." Peers of the realm also have barred helmets, but theirs are silver, decorated with gold, and shown in profile. Baronets and knights have helmets with visors; these are steel, decorated with silver and shown facing forward with visors raised. Mere esquires and gentlemen either have closed visorless helmets or helmets with the visors down. These are of steel and are shown in profile.

In general, most coats of arms displayed today use the esquire's helmet, as shown in the blank coat of arms pattern in Chapter 14.

Some achievements have more than one helmet. Given the importance of helmets in medieval Germany, it is not surprising that it is here that this custom arose. It could be argued that since a man has only one head, there is not much point in displaying more than one helmet. But each helmet, as Dr. Neubecker points out, "represented a right, which was also represented on the shield."[15] As with almost every other element of heraldry, rules about helmets varied from country to country. It is not unusual for a German coat of arms, for example, to display as many as twelve helmets. The British, perhaps being somewhat more restrained, rarely if ever have more than two helmets on their coats of arms. Indeed, there are some authorities who claim that a helmet is not generally included in a heraldic achievement unless it is needed for the placement of a crest (which we shall be discussing shortly). Nevertheless, most commercially produced coats of arms these days include the helmet, probably because the producers believe it makes the achievement look more medieval and traditional. But, in fact, the helmet is something of an anachronism in modern heraldry, and I question the need for its inclusion, not only in newly assumed arms but in hereditary arms. (Unfortunately, this thought occurred to me some time after my own coat of arms, used here as the frontispiece, was painted.)

CROWNS AND CORONETS

Frequently, one sees a coat of arms that has a crown or coronet in place of the helmet. Obviously, these traditionally depicted royalty. The different styles and patterns of helmets are nothing as compared to the variety of crowns. In some instances, there are crowns on top of helmets.

There is no excuse for someone who is assuming a coat of arms to substitute a crown for a helmet unless he or she is of direct royal lineage. Anyone else who does so is pretentious, deceptive, and exercising execrable taste. Under certain circumstances, however, crowns and coronets may be included as part of the design *on the shield itself*. Those circumstances will be discussed when we come to designing your own coat of arms.

ECCLESIASTICAL HEADGEAR

The clergy generally do not use helmets in their coats of arms. Bishops replace the helmet with the bishop's miter, cardinals with red hats, and various church officials use hats of different colors with different numbers of tassels hanging from them. The color of the hat and the number of tassels denote the specific office. The hat is the broad-brimmed pilgrim's hat (see Figure 12).

THE CREST

It is a clear mark of heraldic ignorance when someone uses the term "crest" when referring to a coat of arms. Beware of heraldic merchants offering to sell you "a family crest."

In heraldry, the crest is simply a device affixed to the top of the helmet. As with most of the components of an achievement, it has practical and utilitarian origins. One can visualize some fairly close combat in which one knight attempts to deliver a blow to his adversary. He raises his sword or battle ax high and comes down hard, hoping to strike his opponent on the top of the head and, with a little luck and a lot of energy, perhaps splitting him in two. It made eminent sense, therefore, to reinforce the top seam of a helmet and place something on it that would deflect such a blow. In the fourth century B.C. in the Persian Wars, the Greeks were already using crests, made of feathers or horse hair.

By the late twelfth to early thirteenth centuries, some knights began to appear on the battlefield with fanlike plates standing up on the top of their helmets, probably intended to deflect or reduce the impact of a descending weapon. Given as they were to personal adornment, it was not long before decorations were engraved on these plates.

Over the years crests have evolved into ornamental figures placed on top of the helmet, not unlike, in some instances, the hood ornaments on automobiles. Generally, a crest is an addition to the original coat of arms, given by the heraldic authority acting on behalf of the ruling monarch, to reward the recipient for some special favor or distinction. These days, however, many coats of arms carry crests simply because someone along the line thought they looked nice (Figure 7).

FIG. 7. Helmet with mantle, torse, and crest.

Often, the crest is a repetition or variation of one of the designs in the shield. In Victorian days it became the custom to use the crest, along with some kind of ornamental decoration, as part of the design for household badges which were worn by servants and adorned vehicles, stationery, and other possessions. It is from this practice that the terms "crest" and "coat of arms" are frequently— but always incorrectly—used interchangeably.

THE MANTLING

The mantling, or *mantle,* according to popular belief, owes its origins to the steamy climes of the near East. As mentioned in Chapter 1, a piece of cloth was placed over the helmet and the back of the neck, ostensibly to deflect the hot rays of the sun, which could easily turn a metal helmet into a small oven. It was also fashionable in the Middle Ages to wear a long cloak, called a mantle, which was affixed to the shoulders and hung down nearly to the floor. It was worn by both women and men, and women's mantles often carried heraldic designs. In heraldry, the mantling is highly stylized and in most modern achievements resembles acanthus leaves.

In many royal arms of Europe the mantling is replaced by what appears to be a tent. That, in fact, is precisely what it is. It derives from the canopies that were found over the thrones of monarchs and church hierarchy. Its origins are also in the tents in which the high nobility lived when engaged in military campaigns or sporting activities. These tentlike depictions are known as *pavilions,* and usually appear only in the arms of monarchs and immediate heirs to the throne.

A variation that became popular, particularly in Scandinavia around the seventeenth and eighteenth centuries, were the *robes of estate,* which appeared in the heraldic achievements of officials and dignitaries and resembled or were patterned after the robes they wore in public or when fullfilling the duties of their offices.

To my knowledge, no modern coats of arms have been granted or assumed that include pavilions or robes of estate; it would probably be considered presumptuous to do so. There are other and better ways to indicate one's office or profession, as we shall see in Chapter 6.

THE TORSE

According to popular belief, the torse (also called a *wreath*) originated from the custom, during tournaments, of ladies throwing their kerchiefs to those knights on whom they were putting their money. Each knight would collect the scarves of his admirers, twist them together, and tie them, ropelike, around the crest of his helmet.

Heraldic purists find objectionable an achievement that shows a crest sitting on top of the torse; the crest should always seem to be rising out from it. Crest or no crest, the torse is always shown holding the mantling to the helmet. Attitudes toward the torse seem to vary: In one beautiful little heraldry volume depicting hundreds of coats of arms from all over the world, the torse seems to be as absent as it is present.[16]

Some older achievements have, in place of the torse, a *chapeau,* also known as a *cap of estate* or *cap of maintenance.* As the terms imply, these caps were of varying shapes, styles, and colors, depending on the office held by the wearer. Chapeaus are almost never used in modern achievements, whether granted or assumed.

Another replacement for the torse that is sometimes seen is a crown or coronet that was appropriate to the title or office of the holder of the achievement. As mentioned earlier, crowns and coronets should not be used except where nobly appropriate.

SUPPORTERS

Supporters are figures that usually stand at either side of the shield, holding it up (although sometimes a supporter is a single figure standing behind the shield and clutching on to it for dear life). Where the granting of arms is controlled by heraldic authority, supporters are included in the grant; otherwise, they may not be used. From time to time, monarchs have "awarded" supporters (as well as crests and other so-called *augmentations*) to commemorate a special event or achievement. Individuals assuming arms may choose to avoid supporters in the interests of simplicity.

Supporters may be angels, human figures, or virtually any kind of beast, fish, or fowl, real or fanciful. They may be the same—such as two lions in similar positions—or they may differ, as in the Royal Arms of the United Kingdom with their famous lion and unicorn.

Because supporters depict singular achievements by the individuals to whom they are awarded, they are often colorful, to say the least. Among the British peerage, there is a coat of arms whose supporters are two Bengal Lancers; yet another has two Canadian Indians; there is one with a Tartar soldier and a Matabele Zulu;

others include a Mexican peon, two electrical mechanics, a pair of gate porters of the Bank of England, dragons, peacocks, a rhinoceros, and—one of my personal favorites—the coat of arms of Lord Beaverbrook, supported, as one might have guessed, by a pair of beavers.

THE MOTTO

Strictly speaking, the motto is not part of the achievement, because it is by no means permanent. Those who inherit a coat of arms may keep the motto as it is, change it, or discard it.

The motto can be in any language, although in English heraldry in particular, English, French, and Latin seem to be favored. It is usually displayed on a ribbon underneath the shield and is an expression of morality, religious devotion, loyalty, or patriotism.

Because the motto is not officially recognized as part of the achievement, I recommend that you cheerfully lift and adopt or adapt any motto you come across that is to your liking. Some of the best mottoes I have seen can be found on the crest badges of Scottish Clans. For example: "Danger is sweet" (Macaulay); "I will never forget" (MacIver); "Quite ready" (Murray); "Follow me" (Campbell of Breadalbane); "I am fierce with the fierce" (Chisholm); and, my personal favorite, used by MacPherson, Mackintosh, and several others: "Touch not the cat bot a glove" ("Don't touch the cat without a glove"). One would have to think twice before willingly engaging the enmity of clans carrying such mottoes.

DIFFERENCING

Heraldry is practical. Early in the game, a certain emotional conflict became apparent. On the one hand, a coat of arms was to be considered unique to its owner and jealously guarded and protected. On the other hand, it would seem to be an excellent method of depicting various connections and loyalties. A son, for example, could not inherit his father's coat of arms until his sire passed on to that great tournament in the sky; nevertheless, he would want to proclaim his kinship to the world at large. The same was true of *armigerous* (arms-bearing) personages who wanted to show other familial or patriotic ties. This was easily accomplished by a system known as *differencing,* a procedure that retained all or most of the elements of the original armiger's coat of arms but, as the term implies, with a difference.

In English heraldry, there developed a system known as *marks of cadency.* These are a group of symbols placed over the father's coat of arms with a particular symbol for each son. The eldest uses a *label,* the second a *crescent,* the third a *mullet,* the fourth a *martlet,* etc. The fecundity of our medieval ancestors is evidenced by the fact that marks of difference are cited for as many as nine sons (see Figure 8). In Scottish heraldry there is also a complicated procedure for differentiating the arms of offspring by a series of *bordures* (borders around the shield). When the eldest inherits the arms, he removes the mark of cadency; all the other sons continue to display their father's coat of arms with the appropriate mark.

J. P. Brooke-Little, Richmond Herald of Arms, has commented that "the absurdity of such a system is manifest and consequently it is more honored in the breach than the observance . . ."[17] Marks of cadency are not much in evidence beyond the boundaries of British influence.

There are other methods as well as reasons for "differencing" coats of arms. Familial ties somewhat more distant than direct paternity, or nationalistic allegiances, may suggest the use of differencing. Such differencing can be accomplished very simply. Among the methods that have been used are an exact duplication of the original arms except for a change of colors. Another is to duplicate all but one of the elements in a coat of arms. Still a third is to superimpose on the original coat of arms some small additional element or design. All have been used, all are fair game, and all are accepted heraldic practice, which should be borne in mind by anyone wishing to devise and assume a coat of arms for one's very own.

MARSHALLING

Although there were complicated rules concerning the inheritance of a coat of arms by women, it was sometimes politically or prestigiously advantageous for a man to display his father-in-law's coat of arms. Furthermore, certain acquisitions of property and domains, either accomplished or hoped for, are depicted in coats of

FIG. 8. **Marks of Cadency**

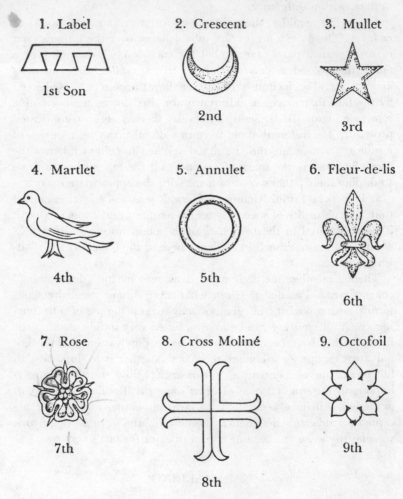

1. Label

1st Son

2. Crescent

2nd

3. Mullet

3rd

4. Martlet

4th

5. Annulet

5th

6. Fleur-de-lis

6th

7. Rose

7th

8. Cross Moliné

8th

9. Octofoil

9th

NOTE: Marks of cadency may also be used as charges.

arms that combine the original arms of the acquirer with those of the acquired. Thus, many of the historical arms of British monarchs include the coats of arms of England and of France. The present-day British royal arms incorporate those of Scotland and Ireland.

There are several methods of combining coats of arms; they all fall under the general heading of *marshalling*. One of the earliest methods was *impalement,* that is, dividing the shield *per pale* (in half vertically) and placing one coat of arms on the dexter side and another on the sinister side. A variation of this technique was *dimidiation,* in which the two coats were bisected with the dexter half of one on one half of the shield and the sinister half of the other on the other half of the shield. It was a technique that soon outlived its practicality, because it not only effectively destroyed both coats of arms, but the combination often resulted in some rather bizarre combinations: ". . . The fanciful charges which it sometimes produced made the life of this form of impalement a short but merry one," writes Brooke-Little.[18]

Toward the end of the thirteenth century, *quartering* became the fashion and eventually became the favorite technique for marshalling arms. In quartering, the shield is divided into four more-or-less equal parts. (The curvature of the lower half of the shield obviates exactly equal partitioning.) If the arms of two families are to be quartered, the one considered most important is placed in the first and fourth quarters. The other arms are placed in the second and third quarters (see Figure 9). As additional arms are acquired, the shield can continue to be divided to accept any number of coats of arms. In some instances, the result is very similar to a badly made patchwork quilt in which individual elements of heraldic design are not only barely discernible, but generally unappealing. Still another method of marshalling is the *escutcheon,* which is another term for a heraldic shield. A small shield bearing the arms of the wife may be placed in the center of her husband's coat of arms; this is known as an *escutcheon of pretence.*

Perhaps the best method of marshalling arms is the simple technique of *compounding,* in which the most prominent elements of two coats of arms are combined to form an entirely different, but nevertheless relevant, design.

Heraldry has been called "the shorthand of history." This is something of an exaggeration: Obviously, not all heraldic designs

FIG. 9. Quartering

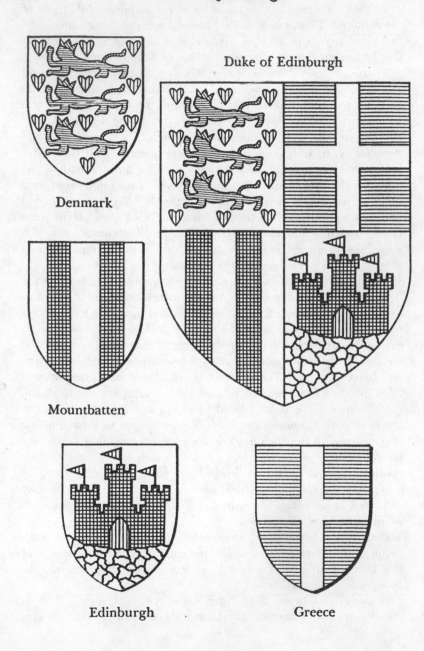

Denmark

Mountbatten

Duke of Edinburgh

Edinburgh

Greece

have historical significance or meaning; some were adopted because of some egotistical or fanciful intent of their originators. Nevertheless, for an accomplished heraldist, marshalled arms can reveal a long and fascinating story. For the casual heraldic observer, they can provide many moments of aesthetic pleasure. Hampton Court, presented by Thomas Wolsey to Henry VIII as a sign of loyalty, has a Great Hall, a vast room that seems to be several stories high. Around the Hall are enormous stained-glass windows showing, among other things, the lineage of Henry's six wives, in the more-or-less traditional family tree style, but using coats of arms. The effect is breathtaking.

TINCTURES

The *tinctures* are all of the *colors, metals,* and *furs* that are used in heraldry. The metals are *Or,* which means gold, and *Argent* (pronounced AR-jint), which means silver. When a blazon specifies these metals, they may be rendered as gold and silver or as yellow and white.

The most common *colors* used in heraldry are:

Gules (pronounced gyoolz)—red
Azure (AZH-yoor)—blue
Sable—black
Vert (vurt)—green
Purpure (PERP-yoor)—purple

Other colors occur in heraldry, but with considerably less frequency. These are *Sanguine* (SANG-win), for blood-red; *Tenné* (TEN-nay) orange; and *Murrey* (pronounced like the name), for purplish-red or mulberry color. Sanguine, Tenné, and Murrey are sometimes called *stains.*

The tinctures of traditional heraldry also include two principal furs: *ermine* and *vair.*

In the Middle Ages, ermine was extremely costly and was, therefore, a status symbol. (Some things never change.) The ermine, a member of the weasel family, has a coat that turns white in winter. It was the fashion to sew the black tips of the animals' tails on to the white fur. This, or a stylized version of it, became the heraldic tincture, drawn as black spots on a white background.

Not content to leave well enough alone, the English devised several variations on the theme: They reversed the colors and called the result *Ermines;* black spots on gold are *Erminois;* and gold spots on back are *Pean.*

A breed of Russian squirrel provided the fur called *Vair.* This hapless beast has a blue-gray back and a white belly, and the skins were sewn so that the colors alternated. In heraldry, therefore, Vair is always understood to be a pattern of alternating blue and white.

There are some who believe that Cinderella's slipper was made not of glass but of fur, and that "vair" was incorrectly translated from the French ("glass" in French is *verre*). It certainly would have made more sense to wear fur slippers to drafty palaces than glass ones which, in any case, would be likely to inhibit dancing.

There seems to be no precise way of drawing the furs; it is usually left to the interpretation of the artist. Figure 10 shows some of the more commonly used patterns for Ermine and its variations and for Vair.

In the seventeenth century a system called *hatching* was devised that is in use to this very day. By means of a series of lines and dots, it is possible to show all of the tinctures in a coat of arms in a black-and-white rendering. To show Argent, for example, the area is left blank; Or is indicated by black dots. The colors are shown by lines going in various directions (see Figure 10 for a complete chart of hatching).

Unhampered by such mind-numbing diversions as television and magazines, the good folk of the Middle Ages allowed their imaginations to run rampant. Almost from its very beginnings, therefore, heraldry was imbued with all sorts of symbolism that had nothing to do with feudal estates, noble rank, or familial pride. By the fourteenth century some heraldists were associating jewels and heavenly bodies with various heraldic tinctures. Or and Argent were, understandably, symbolic of the sun and the moon respectively. Gules represented Mars, Sable was the color of Saturn, Purpure was Mercury's color, Azure stood for Jupiter and Vert for Venus. Or was also the color of topaz, Argent stood for pearls, Gules, of course, meant rubies, etc. And just as the colors of modern national flags are said to represent certain virtues and attributes, the heraldic tinctures were similarly endowed. Thus, Or represented respect, majesty, and virtue. Argent, understandably, was the color of inno-

FIG. 10. **Hatching for Heraldic Tinctures**

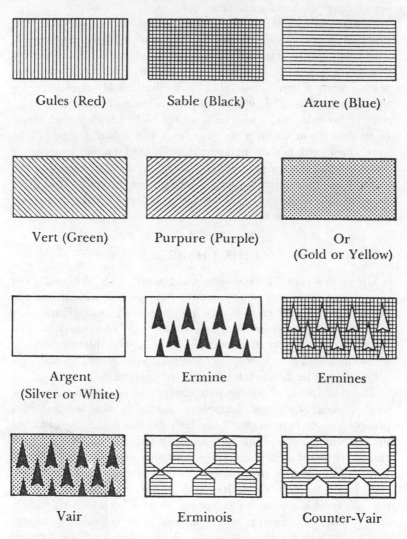

Gules (Red)   Sable (Black)   Azure (Blue)

Vert (Green)   Purpure (Purple)   Or
                                      (Gold or Yellow)

Argent   Ermine   Ermines
(Silver or White)

Vair   Erminois   Counter-Vair

cence and cleanliness. Gules stood for patriotism, Azure for fidelity, Sable, naturally, for mourning, Purpure for royalty, and Vert for beauty, health, freedom and hope. (Other symbolic meanings of tinctures are discussed in Chapter 7.)

Despite such flights of fancy, the medieval heraldists were also practical and from such practicality the *Rule of Tincture* evolved. This rule declares that a color must not be placed on another color or a metal on a metal. The reason is simplicity itself: given the supposed origins of heraldry—that is, on the battlefield—it makes sense that a coat of arms should be clearly visible and discernible from some distance. A gold device on a white or silver background would be as difficult to see as a red one on a black background. (Furs were considered neutral and could be placed on either color or metal but not one fur on another.) It should also be noted that the Rule of Tincture refers to designs against backgrounds. It is quite permissible, and is, in fact, often the practice, to place colors side by side or metals side by side.

THE CHARGES

Up to this point, I have been using words like "designs," "devices," and similar terms to denote the specific patterns on the heraldic shield and crest. These are, however, really inadequate synonyms for the correct term, and should rightly be called *charges*. Briefly, a charge is anything that appears on the shield or on another charge. (Thus, what we have described as *ordinaries* and *subordinaries* are really a subclassification of charges.)

The description of the various charges is far greater than the total number of charges themselves—assuming, that is, that it is possible to even enumerate all the heraldic charges. As we shall see shortly, when properly applied, almost anything can be used as a charge. It then becomes necessary to further describe the charge itself. If, for example, the charge is a lion, the beast can assume a wide variety of positions, each of which has its own specific term. If only the head is shown, it can appear to have been torn off, neatly cut off, with or without a neck, etc., and each method of decapitation has its own specific designation. Rather than lead you through the tedium that a full account of such terms is likely to produce, I recommend instead that you look at the illustrations in Figure 32 for a general idea, and then refer to the Glossary for specifics.

Perhaps a brief look at some of the more common and popular charges will assist in stirring your imagination when it comes to selecting charges for your own coat of arms.

The Cross. Religion, geometry, and the manner in which shields were braced and reinforced all combined to make the cross one of the most popular charges in heraldry. When the word *cross* is used by itself, it refers to a *fess* (a broad horizontal band) and a *pale* (a broad vertical band). This version of the cross is considered one of the ordinaries. Variations on the theme abound. The maltese cross and the swastika are but two variations. The ends of the cross may be rounded, pointed, curlicued, adorned with flowerlike append-ages, etc. Many—but by no means all—variations of the cross may be seen in Figure 11 and some are described in the Glossary.

The three best reasons for including a cross or a crosslike design in a personal coat of arms are religious, aesthetic, and *canting* (a term used to describe a charge that is a pun on the armiger's name; see Chapter 6).

The Lion. If one were to examine an armorial map of Europe, it would become evident that, along with the eagle, the lion is the most popular armorial beast. Lions, long recognized as symbols of courage and nobility (two attributes which modern zoologists have somewhat mitigated), can be found on coats of arms all over the British Isles, France, Switzerland, and in profusion throughout Bel-gium and Scandinavia. In addition, lions appear in thousands of individual coats of arms, including my own. Originally, the heral-dic lion was always shown in the same pose; erect, with a hind paw planted firmly on the ground while the other three menacingly claw the air. The tail is erect and the head is shown in profile. This is known as a *lion rampant.* But soon lions were shown standing, sitting, facing forward, looking over their shoulders, the body in profile and the face full forward, sometimes with two tails, some-times with two heads, sometimes with one head and two bodies. In addition, lions may have collars and chains around their necks, they may be clutching weapons or they may be wearing crowns or coronets. Lions have been merged with other creatures and many are shown as hybrids, having the head and forepaws of a lion with

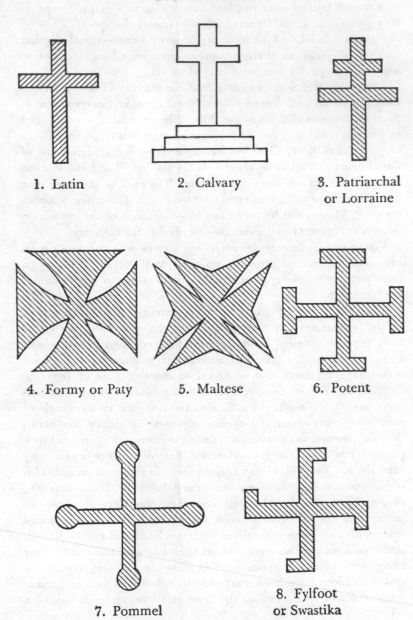

FIG. 11. **Crosses**

1. Latin 2. Calvary 3. Patriarchal or Lorraine

4. Formy or Paty 5. Maltese 6. Potent

7. Pommel 8. Fylfoot or Swastika

9. Crosslet

10. Crosslet Fitchy

11. St. Anthony's or Tau

12. Fourché

13. Pointed

14. Avellane

15. Clechy

16. Patonce

17. Quarter
Pierced

18. Voided

19. Parted and
Fretty

20. Moliné

21. Recercely

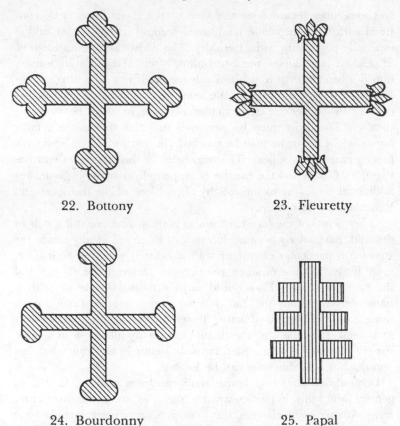

22. Bottony   23. Fleuretty

24. Bourdonny   25. Papal

the hindquarters of a serpent. Lions have even been shown with various parts of the body borrowed from the human figure.

Beasts: Real. A veritable menagerie of animals can be found in heraldry. The same terms that apply to the poses of the lions also apply to most of those of the other animals.

Some slight confusion arises from the fact that the names of real animals were, in the early days, given to fanciful creatures or incorrectly assigned to other animals. In early heraldry, for example, the *leopard* referred to a lion in the *passant guardant* position; that is, three paws on the ground, a front paw upraised, and the face turned forward.

Among the animals that appear in heraldry is the bear, which was sometimes regarded as the king of the forest (not to be confused with the lion, whose traditional domain is the jungle) and is especially popular in Swiss heraldry. The Swiss canton and town of St. Gallen are named for St. Gallus, who, according to legend, tamed a bear to help him build a house. It is not surprising, therefore, that a bear appears in the arms of St. Gallen. There is, according to Neubecker, a particular problem in using bears heraldically. "The artist must be prepared to paint the animal's male organ bright red or he may be mocked (in Switzerland at least) for having painted a she-bear. This was actually the cause of a war between St. Gallen and the canton of Appenzell in 1579,"[19] giving yet additional testimony to the touchy dispositions of the medieval and Rennaissance Europeans.

Other beasts of the forest were also popular and are still much in demand, particularly because so many of them are ideally suited for stressing a particular character trait associated with the animal or, more likely, because of some relationship between the charge and the armiger's name. How could anyone named Wolfe or with a name deriving from the Latin *lupus* (for example, Lobo) resist using a wolf in his coat of arms? Foxes, boars, various kinds of deer and members of the undomesticated cat family all thrive in a wide variety of coats of arms. Elephants and camels are somewhat less popular but with diligence can be located.

Domestic animals also figure significantly as charges. Cattle, in general, and bulls, in particular, are found, as are goats, sheep, and rams. Among ovine charges, the lamb is a particularly popular one because of its religious significance (*Agnus Dei*, the Lamb of God, is an emblem of Christ). Horses and hounds are also frequent occupants of heraldic achievements.

The Eagle. It may be argued (but we will not do so) as to whether the lion or the eagle is the more popular creature in heraldry. The ancient Hittites displayed a double-headed eagle as their national emblem. This noble bird was the emblem of the Roman Empire and was later adopted by Charlemagne as emblematic of his own ambitions toward world conquest. Some indication of the extent of those conquests may be discerned from a kind of loose "circle of arms" that contain eagles. These include both the single- and double-headed variety and may be seen throughout Germany, Austria, Italy, Yugoslavia, Russia, and other countries.

In early heraldry, the eagle was almost always shown *displayed;* that is, facing forward, with its wings outspread and the tips pointing up. Since then, however, a wide variety of positions for the eagle—and for other birds—has been devised. As with the lion, eagles may be shown crowned, and wearing or holding various artifacts. The eagle in the Great Seal of the United States bears a shield on its breast and holds an olive branch in its dexter talon and thirteen arrows in the sinister talon.

Other birds also abound in heraldry. The pelican, for some reason, has gained particular popularity, but it is almost always shown the same way: It stands over its nest and is seen tearing open its breast to feed its young with drops of blood. This rather grisly image is always blazoned as *a pelican in her piety.* Its connotations, however, are religious: it is emblematic of the Eucharist.

Hawks and falcons, indistinguishable in heraldry, appear frequently, either as puns on the armigers' names or as marks of their attributes. Swans, cranes, ostriches, ravens, peacocks, herons, cormorants, roosters, and parrots all serve as heraldic charges. (Surprisingly, *Boutell's Heraldry,* regarded by many as the best basic text on heraldry, makes no mention of owls except to illustrate a particular coat of arms. Other heraldic texts also touch only lightly on this otherwise popular bird, despite its long-standing associations with wisdom and intelligence. It is, however, a legitimate heraldic charge, as evidenced by its inclusion in my own coat of arms.)

A veritable oceanful of marine life swims through heraldry. By far the most popular form is the dolphin, but pike, luce, herring, roach, trout, salmon, eels, and other fish appear in a great many coats of arms, as do cockleshells and scallops.

Even reptiles and insects join the heraldic menagerie, the former being confined mostly to serpents and the latter almost always to bees, although crickets, ants, scorpions, grasshoppers, butterflies, and other insects do occur occasionally.

Beasts: Fanciful. T. H. White writes that "an anonymous person who is nicknamed 'the Physiologus' appeared between the second and fifth centuries A.D., probably in Egypt, and wrote a book about beasts, possibly in Greek."[20] It was this work, expanded and supplemented, that appeared in the twelfth century as *The Bestiary,* and it was enormously popular. It was believed to be an authoritative compendium of most of the creatures extant on the face of the earth. "A bestiary is a serious work of natural history," Mr. White admonishes, "and is one of the bases on which our own knowledge of biology is founded, however much we may have advanced since it was written . . . It can hardly be repeated too often that *The Bestiary* is a serious scientific work . . ." Perhaps we will never fully learn how many of the strange and wonderful creatures that inhabit *The Bestiary* were the result of pure fancy and how many the result of an agglomeration of eyewitness accounts by individuals with limited visual scope, even more limited experience, and influenced by preconceived notions founded on religion and superstition. The fact that *The Bestiary* gained renewed popularity at about the same time that heraldry burgeoned lends still more weight to the argument that heraldry was more than merely an outgrowth of military necessity, but another manifestation of the Renaissance still in its seedling stage, especially since the twelfth century version of *The Bestiary* attributed certain moral and amoral qualities to the animals. In White's modern translation of the book, for example, it is stated: "Because a wolf is never able to turn its neck backwards, except with a movement of the whole body, it means that the Devil never turns back to lay hold on repentance." The ubiquitous lion, on the other hand, will stand up to anybody: ". . . Their courage is seated in their hearts, while their constancy is in their heads." The lion is said to have several characteristics which *The Bestiary* likens to Jesus Christ, who is referred to as "the Spiritual Lion of the Tribe of Judah." How could the medieval heraldists resist?

Of all the mythical beasts appearing in heraldry, the most popular are the dragon, the wyvern, and the griffin.

The *dragon* came to heraldry by way of the Roman army. Although the Romans eventually left the British Isles, the dragon remained as the emblem of those Britons who had resisted the onslaught of the Anglo-Saxons. The heraldic dragon has horns on its head, a forked tongue, a back covered with scales, and armorlike rolls or plates on its chest and belly. It has wings like a bat, a pointed tail, and four legs with birdlike feet, complete with talons. It is almost always depicted *rampant*. It has become the emblem of Wales and appears in several Welsh coats of arms.

The *wyvern* (sometimes *wivern*) is similar to the dragon except that it has only two legs—and those, forelegs; its scaly body ends in a long tail that is usually curled or knotted. It has a horn protruding from its nose. It is usually shown *sejant,* that is, more or less sitting (or as close to sitting as a creature with only two forelegs can accomplish).

The *griffin* (sometimes spelled *gryphon*) is one of those odd combinations of several creatures. Its head, chest, forelegs, and wings are those of an eagle, except that it has ears. Its hindquarters and tail are those of a lion.

The *cockatrice* is a wyvern with the head, comb, and wattles of a rooster.

One of the most popular of the mythical beasts during the Middle Ages was the *unicorn,* which many mistake as simply a horse with a single horn protruding from its head. In "fact," the unicorn was about the size of a goat, and while its head and body resembled those of the horse, it had cloven hoofs, a goatlike beard, tufted hocks, and the tail of a lion. According to legend, the unicorn was fierce, wild, and elusive. It could be captured only when a virgin seated herself in its general vicinity, whereupon the beast would tamely place its head in her lap and could then be readily captured. This was a story that easily lent itself to religious allegory: the virgin was seen as the Virgin Mary and the unicorn as Jesus. Furthermore, at a time when chivalry flourished, the legend of the unicorn showed how strong an influence purity and love could have upon the most wild and untamable of creatures. The beast's horn was believed to contain miraculous powers, including protection against poison. Queen Elizabeth I owned a highly valued drinking vessel made of unicorn horn, and pieces and powders of horns commanded very high prices. Unfortunately, the purchasers were unaware that they were buying the remains of narwhal (Arctic whale) tusks.

The *phoenix* is described in *The Bestiary* as a bird that, when it approaches old age, constructs a funeral pyre, sets itself afire and then, nine days later, rises from its own ashes. To be sure, *The Bestiary* makes the obvious connection between this rebirth and the Resurrection.[21]

The heraldic bestiary includes a wide variety and great number

— May have been our Symbol — not the Eagle!

of what some writers refer to as "monsters." These include Pegasus, the winged horse; the mantygre, which has the body of a lion, the horns of a goat, and the head and face of a man; sea lions and sea horses, consisting of the heads and forepaws of the appropriate beasts and the back and tail of the traditional mermaid. Mermaids and mermen were also sometimes used.

There are almost as many humanoid monsters in heraldry as there are real and fanciful beasts. Some, such as the centaur, appear only occasionally. The manticore has a man's head, with a beard and three rows of teeth, affixed to the body of a lion. Such creatures are, in my opinion, universally ugly and are best excluded from newly designed coats of arms, with the possible exception of the mermaid, who, in the hands of a decent artist, might be rendered in an acceptable, indeed attractive, manner.

Many of the mythical and fanciful beasts are described in the Glossary; some are depicted among the charges shown in Figure 32.

Flora: A considerable variety of plants proliferate in heraldry but by far the most popular are the lily and the rose.

The *fleur-de-lis* (pronounced essentially as it is spelled, except that *lis* is pronounced "lee") has been so stylized that it no longer resembles anything like a lily. There is, in fact, some speculation that it is actually a version of the iris. It figures significantly in the various coats of arms of French royalty and nobility. For a time, it was part of the royal arms of England, to indicate the intent and desire of the British to dominate France.

There are several legends concerning the origins of the fleur-de-lis, including its presentation to the Frankish king Clovis by an angel in acknowledgment of his becoming a Christian.

Another legend suggests that the fleur-de-lis is a highly stylized version of the three toads that were supposed to have been the coat of arms of the Frankish kings. It is further suggested that this amphibian trio is the origin of the nickname "Crapaud Franchos," by which the Flemings referred to the French, and which the English sailors of the nineteenth century changed to "Johnny Crapaud." This eventually deteriorated to the simple "Froggy." The popular assumption that this nickname derives from the supposed preference among the French for the frog or portions of its anatomy as food is essentially without foundation. (Thus do we see, yet again, that even a cursory investigation into heraldry leads us astray into other, and equally interesting, fields.)

The *rose* in heraldry most closely resembles the dog-rose and is usually shown having five petals. The infamous War of the Roses between conflicting royal British houses refers to the red rose of the House of Lancaster and the white rose of the House of York. Henry VII combined the two into what is now known as the Tudor Rose.

The *thistle* has become the emblem of Scotland. Similarly, the *maple leaf* represents Canada and figures prominently in its heraldry, as does the *shamrock* in the heraldry of Ireland. In general, virtually any leaf that can be easily stylized and represented in more-or-less silhouette form can be used for heraldic purposes.

Of a more general nature is the *quatrefoil*, which, as the name suggests, is a simple floral design of four leaves. Variations on this theme are the *cinquefoil* (five leaves), the *trefoil*, etc.

Miscellany: As a practical matter, virtually any object can be used as a heraldic charge. (Whether it can be done with taste and general adherence to heraldic tradition, however, is another matter, which we shall discuss in Chapter 7.) The rule is that the object be readily distinguishable in two dimensions.

More for purposes of example than as an attempt to render a complete catalog, here, by broad category, are some of the objects that now exist in coats of arms.

Tools and weapons: bows, arrows, axes, bombs and grenades, gauntlets, croziers, halberds (a combination of an ax and a spear), hammers, keys, knives, spears, spurs, swords, torches, and tridents.

Nautical and marine objects: galleys, Viking ships, square-riggers, paddle-wheelers, anchors, oars, and rudders.

Clothing: The *maunche*, a sleeve with an elongated cuff, possibly for carrying prayer books, was a popular style at the time heraldry flourished and therefore appears very often as an armorial charge. Of course, crowns, coronets, and helmets also appear with considerable frequency. Chapeaus, designating various titles or offices, appear less frequently. More mundane articles of clothing or adornment can also be found: buckles, rings, and even one achievement with stockings.

Architecture: Castles, gates, and gateways appear in abundance.

The portcullis, a gate with horizontal and vertical bars and pointed ends, is an especially popular charge. The castle usually has two towers, but the charge of a *tower* indicates a single tower. (It should not be confused with the *chessrook,* which is stylized by two curved projections at the top to avoid its being mistaken for the heraldic tower.)

Musical Instruments: Bugles, horns, bells, and harps adorn various coats of arms. One of the more fascinating musical instruments is the so-called *clarion* (also known as a *claricord* or *sufflue*). It is apparently a wind instrument roughly resembling the pipes of Pan but it takes various forms in heraldry. "It has been confused," says J. P. Brooke-Little, "with a lance-rest . . . and even . . . an organ rest, a term which makes confusion worse confounded."[22]

Heavenly Bodies: The sun, moon, stars, and even the terrestrial globe are all used as heraldic charges with considerable frequency and in various forms. They are particularly prevalent in *canting* arms (arms which are puns on the armigers' names). The *sagittary* is a seldom shown charge consisting of a centaur with a drawn bow. As far as I can determine, this is the only zodiac sign that appears with any frequency at all in heraldry—with the exception, of course, of Leo, which appears as a lion in its own right rather than as a zodiac symbol. According to Brooke-Little, "the astronomical signs of the zodiac are sometimes used as charges," but these are rather boring symbols and have none of the appeal of the pictorial versions of the various signs. I have been unable to determine why the zodiac has been so ignored, but I recommend that this situation be corrected by those designing their own personal coats of arms.

The list of heraldic charges is, quite literally, endless: As has been previously mentioned, anything can serve as a charge. Accountants have used the abacus; judges and lawyers have used scales; educators, scholars, and writers have used books both closed and open; the Lamp of Knowledge is probably the first charge that occurs to any educational institution when it thinks of designing a coat of arms; in addition to the ubiquitous cross, the Egyptian Ankh and the Jewish Star of David share in popularity with the Crescent of Islam. A number of charges are illustrated in Figure 32 and more are described in the Glossary. But by definition, there will never be a complete list of heraldic charges. There will always be one more that no one else has ever thought of.

THE BLAZON

The word *blazon* may be used as a noun and a verb. Its simplest definition (as a noun) is that it is a heraldic description of a coat of arms, or (as a verb) to describe heraldically a coat of arms. The blazon is a kind of heraldic shorthand, best demonstrated by example. In ordinary English, the Grosswirth coat of arms (frontispiece) would be described as follows:

A shield divided into three parts in the form of an inverted Y. In the first section, on a white background, an owl with its body facing to the right and its head facing forward, colored black with red beak and claws. In the second section, against a blue background, a gold lion standing upright facing to the left, with a red tongue and claws. In the bottom section, on a red background, an open book properly drawn, with gold binding and clasps and blue edging. Motto: *Nolite Facere Victimas* ("Make no victims").

Now, compare that with the blazon for the same coat of arms:

Tierced per pall reversed; first Argent an owl turned to the sinister side full-faced Sable beaked and membered Gules; second, Azure a lion rampant Or, armed and langued Gules; third Gules an open book proper, bound and clasped Or and edged Azure.

Clearly, a properly written blazon is much shorter and very precise.

There is little argument against the complaint that the language of heraldry has become extremely complicated; some believe unnecessarily so. It is perhaps unnecessary to memorize heraldic lingo except for those seriously interested in delving into the field. Once a coat of arms is designed, a permanent record should be made of the correct heraldic blazon. Once that is accomplished, however, the average citizen will find little use, in ordinary conversation, for terms like *rampant, guardant,* and *rampant reguardant.*

There is a specific sequence in which a coat of arms is blazoned:

1. First, the surface of the shield, known as the *field,* is described —its tincture, its divisions, etc.

2. Next, the principal charge or charges that lie directly on the shield's surface and occupy the most important position.

3. This is followed by the so-called secondary charges.

4. Next are objects that are to be placed on one of the charges that have already been mentioned, such as a crown or a collar.

5. Those charges which are on the field's surface but not centrally situated then follow.

6. Anything placed on the charges in Number 5 is mentioned.

7. Any marks of cadency are last.

These are rather strict rules; however, they should not be considered as holy writ. In general, the two points to be remembered when writing a blazon is that the various components should be listed in order of importance and of sequence. If a shield is divided into a number of compartments, the blazon describes the shield from left to right, starting at the top, like a printed page.

Some of the niceties of blazoning can be tedious. For example, one is not supposed to repeat a tincture if it has already been mentioned. Thus, if a charge has the same tincture as the field, instead of repeating the tincture, the charge is described as being "of the field," or "of the first." In the same way, a charge is said to be "of the second," "of the third," etc. Knowledge of this technique may be useful if you are reading someone else's blazon. In preparing your own, however, I recommend that you ignore it. Feel free to repeat the tinctures as necessary.

With a little practice, blazons are fairly easy to read. Here, for example, is the blazon for the coat of arms attributed to one Major Lewis Burwell who settled in Virginia in 1640: *Paly of six, Argent and Sable, on a bend, Or, a teal's head, erased, Azure.* The crest is blazoned: *A lion's gamb, erect and erased, Or, grasping three bur leaves Vert.* This gives us a picture of a shield with six vertical stripes alternating white and black. Diagonally across the shield from upper left to lower right is a gold band on which is the blue head of a teal cut off at the neck. The crest is the upright paw of a lion, cut off below the knee, colored gold, and holding three green leaves. Here is another, attributed to a William Johnson, who settled in New York in 1742. Arms: *Gules on a chevron, between three fleurs-de-lis, Argent three escallops of the field. Crest: An arm, couped at the elbow, erect, holding an arrow: proper.* This shield has a red background with a chevron, i.e., a wide inverted V painted white or silver. On either side of the chevron's point and at the base of the shield is a silver fleur-de-lis. On the chevron itself are three red scallop shells.

(All of the terms mentioned in the above blazons are defined in the Glossary.)

If however, writing a blazon seems more difficult and complicated than it is worth, you have two alternatives. First, simply write the description of the coat of arms in plain English, using such heraldic terms as are applicable and easy for you to understand, such as the names of the charges. It may not please the heraldic nitpickers, but there is certainly no mistaking a blazon that reads: *On a shield divided into quarters: First quarter, a silver star on a blue background; second quarter, a blue lion rampant on a white background; third quarter, same as second quarter; fourth quarter, same as first quarter.*

The other alternative is to "trick" your coat of arms. This is not only simple but is a recognized and accepted method of "describing" a coat of arms. In tricking, the achievement is sketched as best you can. It need not be an artistic accomplishment; the various elements need only be recognizable. Simple stick figures will do. The tinctures are then written on the backgrounds and charges, usually using the approved abbreviations. (Abbreviations are given for each tincture as part of its definition in the Glossary.) If the charge or area is too small to accommodate the writing, simply write the tincture outside the edges of the shield and draw a line from the tincture to the object or area to which it applies. This is known as a *trick of arms.*

Generally, the mantling is never blazoned unless it differs from custom, which dictates that it consist of the major color and metal of the shield. The helmet also is not blazoned unless it, too, differs from accepted traditional form. The torse carries the same tinctures as the mantling.

Despite all the details that we have discussed in unbuttoning a coat of arms, only the surface has been touched. This realization, however, should not discourage a would-be armiger. On the contrary, it speaks well for heraldry on two counts: first, it proves that heraldry is open and receptive to all levels of interest, from the casual observer to the dedicated careerist. Second—and in the context of this book, more important—it shows what a very wide range heraldry affords for the lively imagination.

Your imagination will be your major asset in developing a coat of arms. It may not be necessary, however, to employ it. There is always the possibility that you are entitled to display an inherited heraldic achievement. Let us now consider that possibility a bit further.

4

Your Own Coat of Arms—Maybe

In general, it is reasonably safe to assume that whether you are "entitled" to a coat of arms is more a matter of custom than of law. One would assume that legal strictures would be most rigid where monarchies still prevail. One would assume incorrectly; the heraldic "laws" of Holland and the Scandinavian countries, for example, are so loose as to be virtually nonexistent.

Great Britain is another matter. Probably the most clear-cut description of the British attitude toward heraldry is given by J. P. Brooke-Little:

> The first [law of arms] is that arms may not be assumed at will but must be the subject of a lawful grant of arms made by a competent authority. Arms are in the nature of an honour rather than a piece of personal property. If the latter were the case then the common law which governs the inheritance of property would have to take cognizance of arms . . . The second proposition is that once arms have been granted they may be borne and used by the grantee, as his especial, personal mark of honour and likewise by his legitimate descendants in the male line . . .[23]

It is only in the British Isles, however, that such strict adherence to heraldic principle is maintained.

Mr. Brooke-Little paraphrases the preamble to a number of

grants of arms made by the Garter King of Arms, John Smart, from 1450 to 1478. This preamble specifies that the arms granted are "signs of honour and gentility." It is perhaps from these honorary and honorable grants that the association of heraldry with a kind of snobbery has arisen. C. Wilfrid Scott-Giles, in his delightful spoof, *Motley Heraldry,* writes, as part of his "Guide to Grantees":

> If, aspirant to arms, you seek
> The heralds in their hall antique,
> It will not get you on their books
> To go there in a Rolls de luxe . . .
> You will be asked to make your claim
> In formal terms; and if your name
> Is Fullovitch or Schtinkenheim,
> Or if you own to doing time
> For murder, piracy or arson,
> Or sending postcards to a parson,
> With courtesy he'll make it plain
> That you need never call again.

Mr. Scott-Giles then proceeds to explain the kind of subtle investigations that the heralds will perform, "plumbing the frightful Freudian chasms/Beneath your mild enthusiams." After more questions and some discussion as to what your coat of arms should include:

> If you survive this searching test
> The clever heralds will digest
> All they've extracted by their guile
> Into heraldic form and style;
> And on a parchment, fairly dight
> With blazonry and seals, they'll write
> Each charge and tinct particular . . .[24]

Clearly, then, British heraldry is subject to some very strict regulations. The extent to which these regulations can be enforced, however, can best be demonstrated by the fact that in several locations throughout the British Isles, including London's fashionable Bond Street, are establishments offering, believe it or not—and to the dismay of the heralds and heraldists—"a coat of arms for your family name." In short, the laws exist so that anyone who normally assumes the arms that belong to another could probably be forced to make some sort of remedy and to abandon the arms. In practice, however, with the exception of the violation of trademark or copyright laws, virtually anybody can assume arms.

In one respect, however, English heraldic law is not only rigid but rigidly enforced. You have no doubt seen commercial firms advertising themselves as being purveyors to the ruling monarch or some member of the royal household and displaying that personage's arms. According to Boutell, it is "an offence for a person acting in the course of a trade or business to give a false indication that goods or services supplied by him are of a kind supplied to any person. The use of armorial bearings to give a false indication of this kind may also give rise to an offence."[25] In such an instance, therefore, it is not so much a case of unlawful heraldry as it is one of misleading advertising.

The College of Arms recognizes its own limitations. In a memorandum in which it discussed its own Court of Chivalry, the College stated that "every kind of misuse of arms is in principle actionable in the Court of Chivalry. A demand for the legal protection of armorial bearings seems at present to arise mainly in case of commercial misuse, and new and simplified protection against the forms which this may take has been provided by the acts of Parliament . . . these may turn out to provide all that is in practice required." The Court of Chivalry has never been called into session, and Brooke-Little questions whether Parliamentary time would be devoted "to place this particular court on a statutory basis."

Great Britain is not alone in maintaining governmental agencies that deal with heraldic matters. South Africa, Ireland, Belgium, Spain, the Netherlands, Finland, Sweden, and Denmark all have heraldic authorities, but they deal mostly with matters involving state and local governments. In general, no one much cares if a coat of arms is assumed. That could be because of a gradual change in the attitude toward coats of arms. These days, they do not carry the significance of honor and distinction they once did— at least not among the common folk. L. G. Pine relates the tale of the British ambassador to the United States in the 1800s who rode around Washington in a carriage adorned with his coat of arms. Once, when the carriage was in the repair shop, a visiting American noticed the adornment, admired it, and as Mr. Pine claims, "proceeded rapidly to bestow on the Ambassador the flattery of imitation." Soon, about a half-dozen carriages, all decorated with the British Ambassador's achievement, could be seen all over Washington.[26]

If the British Isles represent the epitome of heraldry for the nobility and gentry, then Switzerland and the Netherlands must vie for championing the cause of heraldry for the common folk. In the Netherlands, the nobility's armorial bearings are covered by laws against their misuse and assumption by others. Otherwise, anyone at all can assume arms and during what is known as "the republican period" (1581–1815), nearly everyone did so. Rules concerning the use of helmets and supporters are non-existent.

In Switzerland, "practically every parish and every farming or bourgeois family has its own coat of arms and uses it, the ancient traditions of democracy no doubt being the basis for this," observes Carl A. von Volborth.[27]

In France, anyone may assume a coat of arms as long as those arms do not already belong to another, in which case, the usurper may be subject to some legal action. Exactly how this would be accomplished, however, remains something of a dilemma as there are no structures for supervising and registering coats of arms.

The same is true, to some extent, in West Germany. Municipal and civic arms are fairly well controlled, but personal and family arms may be assumed at will—again, as long as they are not in use by another.

On the Iberian Peninsula, the custom of taking the mother's surname as part of one's own extends to the use of coats of arms, so that the rule of descent following only the male line is not applicable. Legally, no one in Spain may display a coat of arms that has not been registered with the *Cronista de Armas,* "heraldic registers." On the other hand, anyone requesting such registration will receive it. (The *Cronista* will also register arms of foreigners residing in former Spanish colonies; see Chapters 8 and 13.)

In Portugal the laws concerning the assumption of arms were abolished in 1910, along with the monarchy and the aristocracy. Anyone who now wants to assume a coat of arms can do so, although there are authorities who regulate civic heraldry and the heraldry of professional societies and commercial enterprises.

In general, there are almost no heraldic authorities anywhere in the world with responsibilities or power relating specifically to heraldry. To be sure, virtually every country has some regulation concerning trademark infringement, and as we have seen, some countries extend such interpretation to the usurpation of heraldic devices.

As for the "rules" that have been established through custom and usage, these are nearly as varied from country to country as are other national customs. When you design your own coat of arms, you may want to pay tribute to the country of origin of your forebears by incorporating some national heraldic trait or characteristic. How that can be done is discussed in Chapter 6.

"A coat of arms," von Volborth says, "is inherited largely in the same way as a name is inherited."[28] That is, in fact, a fairly reliable rule of thumb. In general, arms descend through the male line. All of the sons may bear the father's arms with the proper marks of cadency (see Chapter 3). When the father dies, the eldest son removes the mark of cadency from his arms; the others, however, do not. If they wish to have coats of arms without the mark of cadency, they must reapply to the proper authority for a new or modified grant. (In the case of assumed arms, they can, of course, do whatever they wish. Custom and propriety dictate, however, that they ought not to assume arms identical to those of their eldest brother.)

As mentioned earlier, even illegitimate children have the right to inherit arms; these are often distinguished by special charges. Such charges are sometimes called "abatements" because they *abate* (i.e., reduce somewhat) the status of the coat of arms insofar as they indicate that the individual is not "in the legitimate line of succession. It should be noted that the word *abatement* is not used as implying dishonor. There is no such thing as a mark of dishonor in heraldry,"[29] although a defendant in a Scottish divorce case was assigned an abatement for having committed adultery.

There are even some rules and procedures for adopted sons. In England, for example, if an adopted child is the biological son of an armigerous man, then he may use his "natural" father's coat of arms. If ignorance of his father's identity or circumstances suggest a preference for the arms of his adoptive father, however, he must apply for a royal license. If and when such license is granted (which, according to Boutell, it usually is), the adopted son's coat of arms is distinguished by a mark of difference consisting of two interlaced annulets, the ring that is the mark of cadency for the fifth son. It is my opinion that such rules should be stricken and enthusiastically ignored. An adopted child becomes a member of the family and is likely to inherit virtually everything else from his father, including the name; why not the coat of arms as well?

It has perhaps not escaped your attention that so far, we have been talking about the inheritance of a coat of arms by men. According to custom, in general an unmarried woman bears the arms of her father with no mark of cadency. Except under certain special circumstances, she will not get to keep those arms for her very own unless there are no brothers to inherit them.

Probably because of warlike associations, women in the British Isles do not display their arms on shields. Instead, they use a *lozenge,* a diamond shape. Although the lozenge has been in use since the fifteenth century, it is regarded as a not terribly convenient or aesthetic shape for the rendering of armorial bearings. Sometimes, a round or oval shape is used instead.

When a woman marries, she virtually loses the distinction of her father's coat of arms. She is expected to place her family arms alongside those of her husband's, on his shield.

If a woman becomes a widow, she may continue to display the combined arms of her husband and her father, but she must replace the shield with a lozenge, devoid of crest. Should she be so fortunate as to remarry, her first husband's coat of arms are abandoned.

If she becomes separated from her husband by choice rather than by divine intervention, she resumes displaying the arms of her father, again on a lozenge, but this time differenced with a *mascle,* a charge that is technically described as a voided lozenge, i.e., a lozenge in outline form, thereby declaring to the heraldic world that she is both available and experienced.

There are other rules and customs concerning the bearing of arms by women. (Those who hold office, for example, are permitted to display the arms of that office.) Those rules are complicated and boring; furthermore, they are contrary to the basic philosophy of this book. At the risk of being disdained by heraldic purists, I heartily recommend that all the rules concerning the bearing of arms by women be adopted, adapted, or discarded as the individual sees fit. If you are designing a coat of arms for your family, there is no reason why every woman in your family should not display those arms as a member of the family to whom those arms belong. Some women may want to use the *roundel* or *lozenge* shape to disassociate themselves from the militaristic implications of the shield and to retain some measure of individuality. The husband could display the shield, the wife could use the lozenge, and the children could use either, properly differenced. Furthermore, my recommendations for abandonment apply to all the complicated and niggling rules that make it difficult to design and use a coat of arms. Heraldic usages and customs should be preserved when it is feasible and uncomplicated to do so.

When I speak of a coat of arms for a family, I mean for the immediate family. When you design a coat of arms, you should do so in consultation with your spouse and children. There is no need to do so with brothers, sisters, and other relatives. That does not mean, however, that you should *not* do so. It would not be good heraldic practice for two brothers and their families to adopt exactly the same coat of arms because, should that happen, then in a generation or two, you could wind up with an achievement that has as much meaning as "a coat of arms for your family name." It is entirely proper, however, and, in my opinion, desirable, to maintain some familial relationship in the coats of arms of the branches of the same family. This can be done in a number of ways, by having the same coat of arms with some difference—a border, a change of tinctures, an additional charge, etc.

This same technique can be used even if there already exists a coat of arms in your family. By custom, as we have seen, that coat of arms is inherited by the eldest son in each generation. Thus, while one brother may be entitled to display those arms, the others will not be. They are, however, certainly entitled to display variations or "differences" of those arms.

Before making that decision, however, it is necessary to determine whether there is in fact a coat of arms lurking somewhere in your family.

5

The Search for the
Family Coat of Arms

Before discussing various methods of searching for your own legitimate coat of arms, I want to emphasize that the extent to which you conduct your research is entirely a matter of personal taste and interest. Much has been written about the value of finding one's "roots," an endeavor I heartily endorse. In the course of tracing one's genealogy, it is almost certain that if a coat of arms exists, it will be uncovered. But this is not a book on genealogy. (Excellent books on the subject are available; see the Bibliography.) This is a book whose basic premises are: First, a coat of arms is a personal possession which can and should be passed on to one's progeny. Second, everyone ought to have a coat of arms—certainly everyone who wants one. Third, designing a coat of arms is a rewarding and enjoyable activity resulting in a highly personal achievement (in both the ordinary and the heraldic sense). If, therefore, you have the time and the inclination to do extensive research to uncover what may be an existing family coat of arms, then by all means pursue your objective with the relish and enthusiasm it justly deserves. On the other hand, if the project appears at the outset to be too expensive or tedious—or becomes so—then feel free to abandon it and begin designing a coat of arms for yourself and your family.

The chances are that if your family is in fact armigerous, you are probably already aware of it. No doubt you have seen a relative displaying a coat of arms on a piece of jewelry or tableware. Possibly this person simply purchased what he or she thought was an attractive object bearing the coat of arms of a total stranger. On the other hand, it may well be worth making a few inquiries.

The first place to begin is with family documents that may be easily accessible. Such documents as marriage, birth, baptismal, and death certificates, especially those dating from the early nineteenth century and earlier, may carry coats of arms. Property deeds and contracts may also have them. If there is an old family Bible, particularly one that records births, deaths and marriages, in your possession, look it over carefully. You may be surprised to discover a coat of arms either embossed in the binding or somewhere in its pages.

You should not limit your search to a pictorial coat of arms. It is entirely possible that the achievement has been recorded somewhere as a blazon.

Once you have made a thorough search of your own possessions, you may want to check with relatives to determine whether they have any documents, photographs, or other mementoes that either include a coat of arms or make reference to one.

It may come as a surprise to you and those helping in your search to discover that in looking over your ancestral possessions you will be seeing them with new eyes. An old letter or property deed may have a decorated border or a wax seal which up to now has received only superficial and cursory examination. Under a magnifying glass, they could reveal an old and forgotten coat of arms. Lockets, watches, cuff links, pendants, other pieces of jewelry, and silverware which, because of time and usage, may have been worn almost smooth, may also reveal a coat of arms on close inspection.

Old books are another treasure trove. For one thing, one of the most popular uses of coats of arms, to this very day, is in bookplates. If you look on the inside cover or the first page or two of some ancient volumes that you have not looked at in years and are keeping only for reasons of nostalgia or because you think they may someday be valuable, you may be surprised to find armorial bookplates. You may find more than one design, but if you find one that is repeated, chances are it belongs in the family.

Among the best places to look for family coats of arms are cemeteries, mausoleums, and burial vaults. Of course, such places are always connected with grief and sadness; an excursion to a place of burial can therefore be depressing. On the other hand, the distance of time tends to replace such feelings with a kind of fascination as the information revealed by burial markers often presents a historical framework in which to place our ancestors—not as mere names in the distant past, but as real people. Family coats of arms were frequently placed on tombstones and memorials, especially in crypts in churches. Again, the burial place should be examined with great care, particularly if the marker—a tombstone, a plaque, the entrance to a burial vault, etc.—is especially ornate. Amid all the carvings and curlicues there may be hiding an angel or a cherub carrying a shield on which there is a coat of arms. As long as you are on the premises, ask to see whatever burial documents may be available. You may find a description of the casket, for example, which includes a blazon for a coat of arms that has reverently but ill-advisedly been interred along with its bearer. Also, do not fail to examine the markers of those buried near your ancestors. They may be family members with somewhat different names either because of indiscriminate spelling practices or because of marriage. You may not find a coat of arms on your great-grandfather's gravestone, but who knows whether one is engraved on your great-grandfather's brother's stone?

As you search, keep a sharp lookout for titles and their abbreviations; often, such titles suggest that there is probably a coat of arms to go with them. If your are of English descent, you may find the title *Gent.* or *Esq.* (gentleman or esquire) appearing alongside the names of some ancestors. Lately, it has become the custom to use "Esq." as a very formal title of respect, especially for those in the legal profession, but in earlier times, it was used only by those authorized to do so. Spanish and Portuguese descendants should watch for the titles *dom, don* and *hidalgo;* those of French descent should look for *chevalier;* those of Germanic lineage (or from countries where Germanic languages are spoken) are likely to find coats of arms if there is a *von* or *van* in their names.

If you have been unable to locate a coat of arms from the resources readily available to you, you may now want to go somewhat further afield. To do so, it will be necessary to know where your ancestors came from. Depending upon how far back you can trace your family, you can write to the various religious, civic, state, and even national government agencies requesting information about your ancestor. Invariably (with the probable exception of the Iron Curtain countries) you will receive a response. Sometimes, a fee for conducting the search is involved; if so, you will be informed soon enough. Such searches can be extensive and expensive. Whether the time and cost are worth the results is a decision only you can make based on the intensity of your desire to uncover your roots. If, however, your interest is strictly heraldic and you can identify an ancestor of some hundred or two hundred years back, there are heraldic organizations and agencies in almost every major country who will be willing to help. (A list of these will be found in Chapter 13.) These organizations can also supply the names of reputable local genealogists who can conduct searches on your behalf—always for a fee.

Many Americans interested in tracing their families have engaged in the pleasurable activity of combining their vacations with research. In virtually any village or town in Europe to which an American has free access, you will probably find local citizens eager and anxious to help in your search. Because of the strict adherence and governance of heraldry in the British Isles, those of British, Irish, Welsh, or Scottish descent will probably find their labors most fruitful. The College of Arms in London is an excellent place to start, not only for its historical interest and physical beauty, but because of the willingness of the heralds to be of help. Whether they will initiate a heraldic search on your behalf depends on several factors, including cost, but if nothing else, they can steer you in the right direction for conducting your own search. Heraldic agencies and societies in other countries will also be helpful, but do not overlook conversations with venerable citizens of the region, with church officials, museum curators, and librarians.

If you are at a total loss as to where to begin looking, and if your family has been in America for two or three generations, you can probably get an excellent head start by making contact with the Church of Jesus Christ of the Latter Day Saints—the Mormons. Seven hundred feet below the Rocky Mountains, the Mormons are accumulating what will be, they hope, a complete record of human history, containing the names and vital statistics of every human being ever born. To be sure, they are a long way from achieving their goal, but they are making progress. This repository holds nearly a million rolls of microfilm, containing over a billion names, with records of marriages, births, deaths, deeds, probates, censuses, ships' manifests, and an incredible collection of other records. The church's Genealogical Society will assist you in finding your own ancestors among these records, and while the likelihood of turning up heraldic information is, at best, slim, you should be able to find enough about your ancestors to get yourself started on your own track.

The Mormons believe that those who embrace their religion before death will retain their corporeal form "on the other side" and will rejoin their families. As John Stewart recently reported in *Saturday Review*, ". . . it is largely to convert these ancestors, as well as the living, that the Mormon Church is today compiling this human roll call."[30]

As you continue your quest for your own family coat of arms, bear in mind two caveats:

First, as has already been mentioned, watch for variations in the way names are spelled.

Second, remember that there may be variations in the way a coat of arms is depicted. When you see what appear to be several different coats, examine them a little more carefully. You may find that artistic styles have rendered exactly the same coat of arms somewhat differently. The division of the shield and the placing of the charges will be the same, but many variations in how those charges are drawn are possible.

If your quest for a coat of arms proves futile or too tedious to pursue, you may finally be resigned to devising your own. There are several factors that can enter into designing a personal coat of arms. We shall now explore them.

6

Designing Your Arms—Resources

WHAT'S IN A NAME?

You got it from your father, it was all he had to give,
So it's yours to use and cherish for as long as you may live.
If you lose the watch he gave you, it can always be replaced,
But a black mark on your name, son, can never be erased.
It was clean the day you took it, and a worthy name to bear.
When he got it from his father, there was no dishonor there.
So make sure you guard it wisely, after all is said and done
You'll be glad the name is spotless, when you give it to your son.

The foregoing piece of poetry is available "beautifully inscribed on rich antique-goldtone plate—then mounted on 8½″ by 4½″ walnut finish hardwood plaque . . ." The wood alone is probably worth the price. Above the poem is the "family name prominently engraved . . ." If you want one, it is available at this writing for $1.99 from Jean Stuart, Stuart Building, Pleasantville, NJ 08232; no doubt other mail-order firms also have it.

Setting aside any discussion of the poetic quality of the verse and some of the obvious presumptions it makes (not *every* watch "can always be replaced"; a "black mark on a name" has on occasion been erased; the observation that a particular name has passed through three generations untarnished may, in many instances, be more wishful thinking than fact), it is clear evidence that American entrepreneurs, always ready to respond to a need, recognize the importance of a family name.

Most people are fiercely proud of their family names. When I first embarked on a writing career, anticipating fame and fortune, I had toyed briefly with the idea of changing my name to one more easily remembered. I was informed by older and wiser relatives that to do so would incur the immutable wrath of several dearly loved family elders. For a brief time, I compromised by parting my last name down the middle, thereby not only making the name easier to remember, but providing me with the middle name that my parents had neglected to bestow on me. Fortunately, this affectation was short-lived and my name is now whole again.

Despite the increasing use of our Social Security numbers as "universal identifiers," we still cling to our names as the one unique form of individual identity, even though there may be many others —in some cases, thousands of others—who bear the same name. A coat of arms is also a unique form of identity and, unlike many names, it is—at least among those who observe the heraldic code of honor—entirely unique to the individual who owns it. It seems quite natural, therefore, that the two should go hand in hand. When you consider designing your own coat of arms, you should consider the possibility of using your family name as a source of inspiration for at least one of the charges in your design.

In many instances, that can be fairly easy. For example, according to Scottish custom and belief, each of the clans has its own chief, and only the chief is entitled to bear the arms of that clan. However, there is also the belief that anyone who bears the surname of a particular clan is either a member or the descendant of a member of that clan; therefore, "that surname comes beneath the chief's banner."[31] Thus, if one were to apply to the Scottish authorities for an arms grant, he would be expected to present a blazon that referred somehow to the chief's achievement but would not duplicate it, or that would be differenced according to those formal procedures that apply to branches of the chief's family. In designing a coat of arms, you can effectively do the same.

There are several volumes available showing the tartans of the various Scottish clans. One of my favorites is Robert Bain's *The Clans and Tartans of Scotland* (see Bibliography). Each entry includes a history of the clan, its major tartan, and a drawing of the crest badge. A quick perusal of the book reveals that if your name is Mackintosh, a cat would be an appropriate charge for your coat of arms; if it is Maclean, a tower would be entirely fitting; if you are lucky enough to be named Murray, you would be entitled to display "a mermaid holding in her dexter hand a mirror, and in the sinister a comb, all proper." (In heraldry the term *proper* refers not to demeanor but to the depiction of the charge as it would look in real life.)

In an earlier chapter, we discussed how some names were derived from signs and symbols. Because the widespread use of surnames and of heraldry evolved almost simultaneously, there are some instances of such names being derived from coats of arms which were in existence first. Von Volborth states that the names of Hamlet's erstwhile comrades Rosenkrantz and Guildenstern bore such names. The Rosenkrantz family had an achievement that displayed a wreath of roses on top of a helmet; Guildenstern simply means "gold star."

For the most part, however, the reverse is the case: coats of arms tend to be based on people's names. This is a kind of pictorial punning known as *canting arms*. Rolls of arms and other records dating back to early medieval times clearly demonstrate the popularity of canting arms. Indeed, this technique may have been even more popular than we know: The origins of many coats of arms are unknown and at least some of them are probably based on spellings, pronunciations, or meanings that have since been lost to the language.

The principle behind canting arms is disarmingly simple: You determine the meaning of your name and include something in the achievement that is a pictorial reference to that name. For example, the city of Turin has in its coat of arms a bull, from *toro*. The German family von Baum's coat of arms includes a tree (*baum* is German for tree), those of von Hahn include a rooster, and von Speht show a pair of woodpeckers. The coat of arms of Cardinal Felice di Perretto Ricci show a lion holding a twig from a pear (*pero*) tree. The French word *herisson* means hedgehog, and the animal appears in the coats of arms of families named Harris, Harries, Harrison, and variant spellings. Boutell tells us that cats appear in the arms of Keats, Catt, Catton, and Tibbet (an early form of "tabby"). The German word *hirsch* means deer, and deer appear in the coats of arms of people bearing that surname, as well as in those with names that include the syllable *herz*.

A rather charming variation of canting arms is the *rebus*, a word which may be familiar to you from childhood. In modern usage, a rebus is a puzzle consisting of a series of pictures which, when deciphered, reveals a name or a phrase. Rebuses were very popular in the Middle Ages. The arms of the Borough of Oldham contain three owls. The arms of Bishop Walter Lyhart show a recumbent hart. Abbot Islip's achievement shows a human eye next to a slip of a tree and, lest the subtlety of the humor be lost on the viewer, also depicts a man falling out of a tree.

Sometimes canting arms can become something of an intellectual exercise by employing somewhat more subtle influences. Obviously, if your name is that of a celestial body in English or some other language (Starr, Stern, Luna, etc.), it would certainly be appropriate to use an interpretation of that celestial body in your design. On the other hand, if you wish to be a little more obscure, you could manage some rather interesting derivations. If your name is Bear or Behr or Orso, you could use as one of the charges the constellation Ursa Major. (Those named Orsini would probably be more correct using Ursa Minor.) The same holds true, of course, for any name that derives from the name of an animal that has a celestial counterpart.

It must be noted, however, that such techniques can be taken to extremes that border on the ridiculous. In the seventeenth century, a Danish vicar named Peterson decided to latinize his name to *Petraeus*, which is similar to *petra*, Greek for "rock." In what can only be described as an excess of scholarship, he then proceeded to translate *petra* into Syrian, *Thura*. This is similar to the Latin word for incense, and that is why the Thura family coat of arms now includes a censer. The fact that these convolutions were recorded is almost as remarkable as the convolutions themselves.

Yet another source of heraldic charges related to names is the panoply of saints. If your surname is the same as a saint, chances are it can be pictorially represented. Saints Andrew, Anthony, George, Julian, and Patrick all have their special crosses. Other saints are frequently represented by symbols: Mark by a winged lion, Luke by a winged bull, Peter by keys, Paul by a sword, and John the Baptist by the Holy Lamb. Other saints can be represented by symbols of their martyrdom, such as Saint Sebastian's arrows.

In general, initials do not appear much in heraldry. Royal monograms, such as the current British monarch's "ER," heraldically designated as *cyphers,* rarely appear in a coat of arms itself. The closest one usually finds to a monogram is a variation of canting arms. There are some communities and individuals whose names begin with the letter B and who therefore use a bee in their coats of arms. Actually, it is not a bad charge at all: the bee is a symbol of diligence and busy-ness. And, of course, there is its association with honey and all that implies.

There is one more way of incorporating the name in a coat of arms, and it is included here more as a matter of interest than as a recommendation because it is probably difficult to accomplish and because it must be done in the motto which, as has been previously mentioned, is not, strictly speaking, part of a heritable achievement. The District Council of Chichester (England) has as its motto: *Ad Huc Hic Hesterna.* Freely translated, this means: "The things of yesterday are still here." As a sentiment, it strikes me as rather bland, but if you will look closely you will see that this motto has hidden in it the word "Chichester." Boutell offers several other examples: *Ne Vile Velis,* "Form no mean wish," for Neville; *Forte Scutum Salus Ducum,* "A strong shield is the leader's safeguard," for Fortescu; and *Caveno Tutus,* "Safe through caution," for Cavendish.[32]

Family unity and blood ties can be maintained in a rather satisfying manner by consulting with other family members—brothers and sisters who have married and have families of their own, cousins, etc. While I recommend that each such family group should have its own coat of arms, the familial relationship can be depicted by carrying through the same charge. The simple act of getting the whole family to agree on what that charge should be can in itself either accomplish a considerable amount of closeness or indicate, once and for all, where lines of dissent exist. In either case, the exercise could prove useful. Given the seemingly infinite number of variations possible in designing the coat of arms, there should be little difficulty in two or three branches of a family named Sperling, for example, designing different arms but each containing a sparrow.

Still, despite etymological and genealogical efforts, your name may prove difficult—perhaps even impossible—to be pictorially symbolized. The cause is by no means lost. Your occupation or profession may be another source of inspiration.

WHAT'S YOUR LINE?

Occupations, professions, titles, and offices have long been represented in coats of arms.

Almost since the beginnings of heraldry, officials combined their personal arms with those of the institutions or organizations they served. It is a practice that still prevails. The arms may be *impaled* (the shield is divided in half and the personal arms placed on one half, the institutional ones on the other); they may be *quartered* (the shield is divided into four parts, two of which bear the personal arms, and two the institutional arms); or *in escutcheon* (a small shield with the arms of the institution is placed in the center of the personal arms).

Invariably, someone working for a government agency or a church has ready access to some emblem, design, or insigne that is heraldic in character and is adaptable to a personal coat of arms. Unless the individual designing his own achievement holds an extremely high office, it might be considered pretentious to include the entire heraldic-like device in a personal coat of arms by impalement, quartering, or in escutcheon. Still, there is nothing to prevent appropriating a portion or a variation of that emblem. Such insignia of office as military batons, admiralty anchors, swords, and maces have all been used heraldically.

Much more commonplace, however, has been the use of tools of the trade by craftsmen, artisans, and artists. The open book in the Grosswirth coat of arms is equally appropriate for a writer, a printer, a bookbinder, a teacher of literature, a librarian, a publisher, an editor, a book seller, a book collector, or someone whose chief diversion is reading.

Tools may be either highly stylized or depicted *proper*. The venerable arms of the Spectacle Makers' Company of London contain three pairs of readily recognizable eyeglasses (see Figure 1). Since the earliest days of heraldry, smiths have used tongs, hammers, and anvils in their coats of arms. Locksmiths have used locks and keys, as have official doorkeepers, innkeepers, and the various other occupations and professions associated with these devices. (A note of caution: Because keys are available in such a wide variety of styles and shapes, when blazoning the coat of arms, a fairly detailed description of the key should be given. If it is a particular type of key with a specific designation, that designation should be included in the blazon.)

One of the most stylish representations of a coat of arms that exemplifies canting arms, and also includes both tools of the trade and the symbol of office, is the achievement of President Dwight D. Eisenhower. His assumed arms show a blue anvil on a yellow background. (*Eisenhauer* is German for blacksmith.) The crest consists of the circle of stars that is the emblem of a five-star general.

Tools and artifacts, however, are not the only resources for representing a profession or occupation in a coat of arms. Just as heavenly bodies may be employed for canting arms, they are equally useful for occupational representation. Navigators and pilots could certainly depict a representation of the North Star. Astronauts and anyone else connected with outer space would not be remiss in including the moon. Astronomers, of course, could have a veritable field day in the heavenly bodies that could be incorporated in their coats of arms.

Any number of charges are, by association, legitimate symbols for the method by which one earns one's sustenance. A tree could grow on the coats of arms of foresters, ecologists, naturalists, botanists, people in the lumber or timber industry, those who own or manage orchards, operators of commercial nurseries, etc. Similarly, flowers can be cultivated in the arms of anyone whose name or occupation is suggestive of floral representation—including, but by no means limited to, dedicated amateur gardeners.

Architects, real estate agents, decorators, and anyone else involved in housing could certainly use a castle (based on the popular cliché concerning a man's home). Bulls and bears can romp rampant over the shields of zoologists, breeders, and stock market speculators.

Romantics designing their own coats of arms may be interested to learn that the mermaid is a popular charge and can be legitimately included to represent an occupation. For one thing, almost anything involving the sea is fair game for a mermaid. She can be

shown holding anything that refers to a specific occupation, such as
a fishing net. If however, she is blazoned a mermaid *proper*, she
will be shown holding a mirror and comb, immediately making her
available for professionals involved in the often-difficult task of improving the appearance of the general populace.

If it is the intention and desire of the designer of a coat of arms
to represent a woman who is "in all respects an admirable creature,
kind, considerate, generous, and a good mother,"[33] he might consider a variation of the mermaid known as the Melusine, heraldically depicted as a mermaid with a double tail. She comes from
German heraldry and no one seems to know why she is so drawn;
the original Melusine was half woman and half serpent. According
to legend a French count found her one day in the woods and, as
was so commonplace in those days, experienced a case of love at
first sight and pleaded with her to become his wife. She agreed, on
the condition that on Saturdays she was to be allowed to remain
out of sight. The marriage was an extremely successful one, yielding
a number of sons and a considerable amount of power and wealth
for the count. After several years, however, the count was unable to
resist his overpowering curiosity, and one fateful Saturday, spied on
her as she was bathing. He was shocked to discover that from the
head to the navel she was indeed the beautiful creature he had always thought her to be, but from the navel on down, there was the
blue and silver body of a serpent. The count begged his beautiful
spouse to forgive him for spying and she consented, but unable to
leave well enough alone, he referred to her as a serpent, "whereupon Melusine flew out of the window uttering a loud cry of an-
guish."[34]

Admittedly, the legend stretches credibility. How the count was
able to sustain a happy marriage, fathering several sons in the process, without discovering the somewhat unusual construction of her
body below the navel is difficult to comprehend; he must have been
either woefully inattentive or incredibly dense. Indeed, basic physi-
ology suggests that the story is nothing more than a piece of charming fiction. Nevertheless, it has given us a most acceptable heraldic
charge.

While the mermaid and her variations offer genteel associations
in heraldry, the merman usually does not. When he is shown using
a conch shell as a horn and holding a trident, he is blazoned as

Triton, the mythological god whose fearsome breath causes high winds and tempestuous storms. He is considered something of a menace. But Triton is also the name of one of the satellites of the planet Neptune; and in physics a triton is a positively-charged particle consisting of two neutrons and a proton. In modern heraldry, therefore, the merman can successfully be engaged to represent nautical, astronomical, and scientific occupations.

Thus, although your occupation, profession, or office is real enough, the extent to which it may be symbolically represented can run the gamut from stark reality to utter fancy.

You could also use an occupational charge that relates to your name if not your occupation, if the name is of occupational origin. Anyone named Fletcher could show an arrow; Hunter can show a hunting horn; Carpenters could avail themselves of any number of devices, as could all of the carriers of occupational names as discussed in Chapter 2.

And yet, occupations and professions—whether currently engaged in or suggested by the family name—may still fail to yield heraldic inspiration. Rest easy; there are other vast sources to be tapped.

HOME IS WHERE THE HEART IS

The often quoted cliché that only the American Indian is the true native American *is* often quoted, and *is* a cliché because, of course, it is true. Because of the enormous diversity of the American population in terms of origin, each of us has an almost unlimited source of inspiration for designing a personal coat of arms. Each of us can look to our ancestors and their homelands for heraldic inspiration.

An experienced and knowledgeable student of heraldry usually can distinguish the nationality of a coat of arms from its design. Varying styles of helmets may differentiate the coats of arms of one country from another, the shapes of the shields are frequently different, and the kinds of charges and the way they are placed are also indicators of an achievement's origins. Thus, by making a cursory study of coats of arms originating in the country of one's forebears, it should be possible to unearth some characteristic of the design, or a typical charge, that can be pleasingly incorporated in one's own personal arms. For example, the coat of arms for the

Irish Republic contains a gold harp. The Belgian coat of arms contains so many lions that surely no one can object to an American of Belgian descent borrowing one or two. The *fleur-de-lis* is almost always associated with France. The *eagle affronty* is the coat of arms of West Germany. Austria's coat of arms is also the eagle; the imperial Austrians displayed a double-headed bird, while the Republic of Austria has the somewhat more modest single-headed version. Switzerland's arms consist of a simple white cross on a red background. The Kingdom of Hungary had arms replete with crowns, crosses, and crowned lions. Portugal's contain shields and castles. The arms of Spain have castles (for Castile), lions (for León), and for Granada, a rather charming pomegranate. The Czechoslovakian arms have a double-tailed lion rampant; the heirs to the throne of Italy bear a white cross on a red shield, supported by lions; the arms of the Italian Republic depict a star. The royal arms of Denmark are a veritable zoological picture gallery compared to Norway's, which show a simple lion wearing a crown and holding a battle ax. The arms of Poland consist of a white eagle on a red field. Those of Imperial Russia are a hodgepodge consisting of a central shield bearing the arms of Moscow, surrounded by the arms of various cities and provinces, all overlaid on a double-headed eagle. Even the Great Seal of the United States contains a number of elements readily adaptable to one's personal coat of arms.

Let us review some of the characteristics that distinguish the heraldry of those countries that have strong armorial backgrounds. It is respectfully suggested that you look at all of them, even if you are personally interested in only one or two, to gain some positive inspiration before incorporating nationalistic elements in your own coat of arms.

AUSTRIA: See GERMANY

BELGIUM: As already mentioned, it is almost mandatory that a rampant lion be incorporated in a coat of arms that depicts a Belgian heritage. The helmets of Belgian family arms are usually gold, silver, or steel (gray), with grills and edges in gold.

DENMARK: The official arms of modern Denmark include three lions in the *passant* position; i.e., standing on three paws with the right forepaw raised. These creatures date from King Waldemar the Great (1157–82). They wear crowns and are bedecked with hearts. Coronets depict royalty or titles; otherwise there is no difference between the arms of those with and without titles.

FINLAND: Until 1809, Finland was part of Sweden, so its heraldry is similar, and closely related, to Swedish heraldry. The rampant lion wearing a crown and carrying a sword has already been discussed. Also part of the Finnish coat of arms are nine white roses, representing the nine Finnish provinces.

FRANCE: Of course, the most distinguishing feature of French heraldry is the fleur-de-lis. Another unique characteristic is that if an achievement includes a motto based on a war cry, the motto is usually placed over the shield rather than under it. French aristocrats commonly included supporters in their achievements, and while it was considered unusual for untitled persons to do so, there are no inviolable rules in that regard. There were, however, some extremely complicated rules concerning the types of helmets, the number of bars on them, their coloring and positioning. Perhaps the best approach is to ignore these rules and if you decide to include a helmet in your own coat of arms, use the virtually universal British esquire's helmet.

In 1696, King Louis XIV amassed a war treasury by establishing a tax on coats of arms. In a move worthy of any contemporary politician, he then arranged to have coats of arms given to those who did not already have them. As a result, achievements proliferated among the common folk in France, and the arms registry, known as the *Armorial Général,* which is still in existence, records well over 100,000 arms, about 90 percent of which belong to commoners. Maintaining what must be interpreted as some sort of balance between the need for ready cash and the desire for aristocratic aloofness, commoners were not permitted to include helmets and crests in their arms.

French heraldry went out of existence with the Revolution. Napoleon attempted to revive it by introducing his own style, along with a whole new set of rules. The result today is something of a hodgepodge, consisting of pre- and post-Revolutionary heraldry.

GERMANY and AUSTRIA: The history of Germany and Austria is inexorably tied to that of the Holy Roman Empire, founded in 962 when the German king Otto the Great was named Emperor by the Pope. The Empire lasted until 1806 and involved, in addition to Austria and Germany, the Netherlands, northern Italy, and major portions of Poland, Hungary, Bohemia, and the Balkans. This explains why the eagle and the double-headed eagle, which figure so prominently in German and Austrian heraldry, also fly in the heraldry of other European countries.

The Germans are committed to the concept of *Familienwappen,* "family arms," so the tradition of individuals within a family altering their arms is not commonplace in German heraldry. Usually, such differencing, especially among the untitled, is accomplished by changing the colors or the crests. In general, a German commoner's achievement consists of a shield and a tournament helmet and is likely to exclude the mantling, the torse, and the crest.

GREAT BRITAIN: Inasmuch as most of the "general" rules of heraldry discussed in this book are British in origin, it would be redundant—not to mention extremely difficult—to summarize the characteristics of British heraldry in a paragraph or two. If your background is English, Scottish, Welsh, or Irish, you will probably have no difficulty designing a coat of arms by following the regulations and customs generally discussed throughout these pages. (However, see "Scotland" below.)

HUNGARY: From the fifteenth to the eighteenth centuries, the Turks regularly invaded Hungary, practically as a diversion. One result of this Turkish persistence is the appearance of a Turk's Head in many Hungarian coats of arms. He is always depicted with a heavy black moustache and frequently shown wearing a turban. Invariably, one can see the blood dripping from the place where the neck was separated from the rest of the body. According to von Volborth, this gory spectacle appears in "more than 15 percent of all Hungarian coats of arms."[35]

As one who generally dislikes the use of the human figure in heraldry (mostly for aesthetic reasons), I recommend that readers of Hungarian descent eschew decapitated Turks in favor of the rearing horses and cavalry types, which also appear in Hungarian heraldry. Even the human arm, typically encased in armor and clutching in its hand a sword, is preferable to the severed head— but not much. The arms of the Kingdom of Hungary include lions' heads, a six-pointed star, double- and single-headed eagles, and several other much more appealing elements, representing Dalmatia, Croatia, Slavonia, Transylvania, Rijeka, and Bosnia and Herzegovina.

ITALY: The heraldry of Italy is also a reflection of a long history of foreign influences, including those of Germany, France, and Spain. Perhaps the most distinguishing element of Italian heraldry is the shield. The "heater" shield is frequently used in Italian arms, as it is in so many other countries. But also popular in Italian heraldry is the so-called "horsehead" shield, named for its vague resemblance to the shape of a horse's head when seen from the front. Another characteristic Italian design is a kind of almond shape which would be oval were it not for the fact that it comes to a point at the bottom.

There is a complicated set of rules for the use of crowns and coronets by the nobility, but apart from that, there is little to distinguish Italian heraldry except for the torse, which is characteristically painted so thin that it is almost indistinguishable.

Another aspect of Italian heraldry is the appearance, in the chief of some shields, of charges that represent historical political alliances. For example, a black double-headed eagle on a yellow background indicated allegiance to the Holy Roman Empire.

THE NETHERLANDS: Typical of the general goodwill which one tends to associate with the Dutch, anyone can bear arms, and during the Republican Period (1581–1815) a vast number of families assumed arms. With the exception of one or two regulations forbidding the use of crowns and coronets, Dutch heraldry is fairly freewheeling. Lions and crosses abound. There are no rules as to the type, position, or number of helmets. The use of supporters is also entirely up to the individual assuming the arms. Mottoes are not common in Dutch arms except in noble families; this is, however, a matter of tradition and not a "rule."

NORWAY: The Norwegians never got terribly exercised about controlling heraldry. Throughout history, they have not only assumed coats of arms but have freely altered them so that supposedly inherited achievements sometimes bore little resemblance to their predecessors. Even during the Middle Ages it was not unusual for brothers to bear coats of arms that differed from each other's and from those of their father. The royal Norwegian coat of arms is beautifully simple: it consists of a red field against which is placed a gold lion rampant holding an ax. It is clean, elegant, and highly recommended for inclusion in newly assumed arms.

Modern heraldry merchants would have loved the Norwegian

tradition in which an individual could assume the coat of arms of another if the names happened to be similar, especially if the assumed arms belonged to a family that had died out. While this practice is acceptable in Norwegian tradition, it is generally not considered good heraldic etiquette these days.

POLAND: The charges and divisions that are so commonplace in most European heraldry are virtually nonexistent in Polish heraldry. Charges often resemble ciphers and runes, and are not found in any other national heraldry. In some instances, these have evolved to more traditional heraldic forms such as crosses, crescents, horseshoes, etc.

Polish heraldry is complicated by a system unlike that of any other country. An example is the *proclamatio* arms, each of which may be held by more than a hundred families. The arms themselves have a name, invariably different from the family name, and were assigned to groups of families that typically had no relationship with each other. (*Proclamatio* is Latin for "war cry"; this may offer a clue as to why this system was developed.)

Of all the Communist countries, Poland is the only one that still retains its traditional coat of arms—a white eagle on a gold background, a design that dates back to the thirteenth century and was part of the armorial bearings of Polish monarchs. What with the Russians and the Germans vying for domination of Poland throughout its history, it is understandable that much of Polish heraldry was lost in the various attempts to "de-nationalize" Poland.

PORTUGAL: Throughout its history, Portuguese heraldry has been plagued with arguments, primarily between heraldic authorities established by monarchs, and members of the aristocracy who resented any interference with their right to bear arms. These debates continued until 1910, when the Portuguese monarchy was abolished. Since that time, the assumption of arms has been permitted.

Concurrent with the custom of assuming a maternal surname was the practice of assuming the maternal coats of arms. There were rigid rules involving marks of cadency, depending upon whether the arms were of maternal or paternal origin, and persons of Portuguese descent who want to "play by the rules" are probably well-advised to devise brand new coats of arms which allude to ancestral arms through the use of charges.

The current Portuguese state coat of arms is not, I am forced to admit, among my favorites. On a white shield are six smaller blue shields arranged in a cross. Around the white shield is a bordure containing seven towers. The shield is laid over an armillary sphere, an ancient astronomical instrument.

RUSSIA: It was not until some three hundred years after heraldry began to develop in Western Europe that it finally made its appearance among the Russian nobility in the Western part of the country, having drifted across the border from Poland. It took a couple of centuries more for the idea to proceed eastward across Imperial Russia. As a result, Russian achievements, based on an already developed system of heraldry, tended to be relatively free of the simplicity so characteristic of early Western European heraldry. The so-called "small coat of arms" of Imperial Russia, immediately prior to the Bolshevik revolt, consisted of a black double-headed eagle on whose breast were the arms of the City of Moscow and on whose outspread wings were the coats of arms of eight provinces and cities.

In the latter part of the eighteenth century many municipalities that did not already have coats of arms were required to assume them. It was the custom to frame a civic coat of arms with ears of wheat or corn, a wreath of foliage, or green branches, and such charges would be fitting for someone of Russian ancestry to use in his or her own arms. It should be remembered, however, that the modern emblem of the Soviet Union consists of two sheaves bound by a ribbon and encircling a globe over which is laid the hammer and sickle. Variations on this theme are in the arms of many Communist countries.

SCOTLAND: Scottish and English heraldry are very much alike, both in style and in regulation. The Scots are as persnickety about their heraldry as the English are. It is permissible to use a clan's crest badge, but only in certain forms and patterns, which include encirclement by a strap-and-buckle arrangement. The arms or crest of a clan chief or a clan itself probably should not be used in assumed arms. All clans, however, have badges, and while the badge itself should not be used, it is certainly possible to adopt some element of it. A wide variety of animals appears in Scottish crest badges, and any one of these could be used in assumed arms as long as care is taken not to copy them exactly. Changing the position, the tincture, or the way in which the beast is represented should suffice. For example, where the original contains the head of a lion or unicorn, assumed arms could include the entire beast.

SPAIN: Much of what has already been discussed about Portuguese arms is applicable to Spanish arms.

Perhaps the two features that most distinguish a Spanish coat of arms are the bordure and tincture. Possibly arising from the desire to combine the coats of arms of married couples, Spanish shields frequently have a border around the edge. These are usually charged with castles, crosses, chains, or a motto.

Spanish arms also violate the Rule of Tincture, particularly with respect to metals. It is not unusual for Spanish arms to have both white and silver (in most other cases, it is one or the other) or yellow and gold, sometimes in combination. The arms of the city of Soria have a silver bordure with a white motto written on it. Spanish arms do not generally use supporters, but there is no rule against them.

SWEDEN: While some rules pertaining to royal use and placement of coronets and helmets apply, in general, Swedish heraldry tends to reflect its German roots, and has developed more or less along the lines of Danish heraldry. It is replete with lions, crowns, crosses, and most of the usual acceptable charges. (One of my favorite Swedish coats of arms is that of the Goos family which depicts the fowl perched atop a crossbow.)

SWITZERLAND: Swiss heraldry is a reflection of a wide variety of influences—German, Prussian, Italian, French-Napoleonic, and even Hungarian and Bohemian.

Swiss heraldry tends to be clean and uncluttered. An unusual charge particularly appropriate to the Swiss is the *Tellenhut*. During the Helvetic Republic (1789–1803) the Swiss were reluctant to give up their fondness for heraldic achievements. Many families adopted the *Tellenhut*, which is William Tell's Cap of Liberty, and it is an entirely appropriate charge for people of Swiss origin to use on their assumed arms. So is the crossbow and an apple tree.

UNITED STATES: With the exception of the United States Army's Institute of Heraldry, which concerns itself with military matters, there is no recognized heraldic authority in this country. Nevertheless, there is a long-standing tradition of American heraldry. The American flag, for example, is based on the arms of George

Washington (two horizontal red stripes on a white background, surmounted by three red stars). Many American families are, of course, armigerous.

In addition to national coats of arms and emblems, in those countries where heraldry has existed for some time, just about every province, state, city, and town has its own coats of arms. These, too, can be adapted for private use.

If the soil in which your own ancestral roots are planted has not been mentioned here, do not be discouraged. A visit to any public library should make available to you the flags and national emblems of every country in the world. Furthermore, there are many books describing in some detail the coats of arms of various countries, and a little research either in a major public library or in an ethnic library should prove rewarding.

A MEMBER OF THE CLUB

During the Age of Chivalry, there arose a veritable galaxy of knightly orders. Each had its own symbols and emblems, and each of these, in turn, is surrounded by a complex ritual of usage for the members of those orders and their descendants. Since these are not likely to apply to a majority of the readers of this book, there is little point in going into detail about them. However, they suggest a practice that can be readily modernized. If you belong to a society, fraternity, professional organization, or some other group, particularly one in which membership itself is a distinction or in which you have achieved some standing or accomplishment, it would be perfectly reasonable to include some representation of that organization in your own coat of arms. This could easily be accomplished by using some heraldic device from the organization's own seal or official emblem or even a part of its coat of arms.

It should always be remembered that when incorporating the arms or the elements of the arms of a place of origin or of an organization, it should be done in a way that does not duplicate the original arms or suggest that the new arms belong to some member of a modern or ancient nobility or of an official of the government —unless, of course, they do.

7

The Ultimate Achievement

We now come to a matter of some delicacy: good taste.

Someone once defined "good taste" as "anything that pleases me." It is possible to ignore and deliberately violate all of the rules and traditions of heraldry and still come up with a relatively pleasing coat of arms. On the other hand, it is equally possible to rigidly observe all the rules and render an achievement that is an absolute horror.

Insofar as design is concerned, heraldry has certainly had its ups and downs. Toward the end of the Middle Ages, heraldry experienced "a flamboyance of design unknown in previous centuries."[36] During the Tudor period there seemed to be a return to somewhat more simple designs, but about a hundred years later some of the complexities re-emerged. In my opinion, heraldic design reached its nadir during the Victorian era. As mentioned earlier, while a heraldic blazon is fairly specific as to the division of the shield and the placement of the various elements, it can be interpreted in a number of ways, depending on local custom, current style, and the propensities of the particular artist. During Victorian times, excess prevailed in heraldry as it did in most other things. As Brooke-Little points out, late Victorian grants of arms depicted shields replete with curves and curlicues surrounded by heavy gilt frames, "but as the heralds of the day were happy with it, who are we to condemn it on any grounds other than aesthetic?"[37] Who, indeed?

The same is applicable today. The purpose of this chapter then is not to teach or preach aesthetics, but to provide a few guidelines that may prove useful in designing a pleasing coat of arms.

A recent book on amateur genealogy suggested that individuals designing their own coats of arms might want to include a representation of a baseball field (simple enough to do with existing and known heraldic charges) and with a crest consisting of an arm holding a baseball bat and with the motto: "Play ball!" Another suggestion for the sports enthusiast was a shield on which some tennis balls had been placed with the motto reading: "Next year Wimbledon." Suggestions such as these cause true heraldists to have nervous breakdowns.

Essentially, then, what constitutes a good-looking coat of arms is whatever looks good to you. If you adhere to the rules of design discussed throughout this book, you will not go far wrong. In general, a coat of arms should be more-or-less heraldically traditional, it should be in good taste, and should be symbolic of the name, the occupation, the country of origin, or some other quality or characteristic of particular significance to the person displaying the arms. It is, of course, both possible and acceptable to combine several such elements. Aesthetics alone could dictate the elements of a coat of arms: you could include a lion or a horse or a ship simply because you like lions, horses, or ships. Still, because of the heritable aspects of a coat of arms, I much prefer one that somehow represents the armiger.

Your local public library, art museum, or historical or genealogical society can probably provide you with the names of heraldic artists who can paint your coat of arms once you have designed it. However, any reasonably talented commercial artist should be able to render a coat of arms that is quite acceptable. He or she need only refer to a heraldic art book for an idea of what the achievement should look like. *Heraldic Design* by Hubert Allcock is an excellent handbook for artists (see Bibliography). The pattern in Chapter 14 is a fairly standard one for a modern coat of arms and can be used with confidence.

THE SHIELD

As indicated in the pattern, the "heater" shape, revived in the nineteenth century, continues to be the most frequently used outline. However, any of the other patterns shown in Figure 12 are

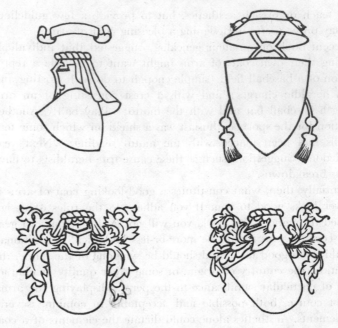

FIG. 12. Variations on the basic pattern for a coat of arms. (At upper right, the ecclesiastical pattern for a Catholic priest).

also acceptable. If you wish to retain a specific shield pattern in your coat of arms, it is necessary to mention that pattern in the blazon. It is, however, not recommended that you do so. Part of the artistic interpretation of a blazon is the right of the artist or whoever has commissioned the artist to specify the type of shield that is preferred.

Now that you are at the point of actually devising a coat of arms, it is necessary to make a decision about whether to obey the long-standing rule that shields are not to be used by women. As you know by now, it is a rule which I recommend violating. Traditionally, women's coats of arms—particularly those of married women or widows—are "properly" displayed in a *lozenge* (diamond shape) or oval. Some may simply find these shapes more aesthetically pleasing. Nevertheless, as one who prefers his heraldry along traditional lines, I recommend again the use of the shield for everyone. If you disagree and want your arms contained in an oval, a diamond, or even a circle, that, too, should be stated in the blazon.

CHARGES

The charges that consist of *ordinaries* usually occupy about a third of the shield; the *subordinaries* occupy about half the space of an ordinary.

A reminder: crowns and coronets should not be used outside the boundaries of the shield unless the armiger is of royal or noble descent. If you are designing your own coat of arms and you place a crown above the shield in lieu of the helmet, then you are also assuming a royal status which, unless you are properly entitled to it, is a notch lower than buying a coat of arms to go along with your name. Crowns and coronets can, however, be included in one of the charges on the shield when appropriate, such as in canting arms (Italian Corona, German Krone) or because it is adapted from a national coat of arms, or because it has some other proper association. Again, in the interests of good taste, crowns and coronets should be kept simple. A somewhat abstract form with as little detail as possible is recommended. Perhaps the best form is a simple representation of a three-pointed crown.

Remember that a crown is made of metal and its tincture should be *Or* (gold or yellow) or *Argent* (silver or white).

As mentioned in Chapter 3, virtually any object can be used as a charge as long as it is readily distinguishable in two dimensions. Thus, my earlier comment concerning the use of tennis balls and baseball bats as unacceptable charges may be legitimately questioned. I have no answer except to say that to me, they are aesthetically offensive. *The Wall Street Journal* once reported that the Crane family of Chicago, who earned millions by producing plumbing fixtures, was offered a new family coat of arms consisting of a shield charged with a bathtub and sink and bearing a crest consisting of a hand pulling a toilet chain. The recommended motto was "*Après Moi le Déluge.*" Displaying the wisdom by which it became rich, the family rejected the offer.[38] (See *Urinal* in the Glossary.)

Recently granted arms in England have included "a representation of the path of two electrons rotating round a nucleus" and another that contains "three representations of the symbol of the para-magnetic electron" (Figures 13 and 14). Perhaps the ultimate decision as to what constitutes a proper charge is the dignity of the device itself, the symbolism it carries, and its relative seriousness. A coat of arms, after all, is something that is intended to last as long as the lineage does; it need not be stodgy, but it ought not to be frivolous either.

One more word about the use of human figures in coats of arms: They are difficult to render, and they tend to be used for religious representations or to illustrate the defeat of some group. Again, while it is a matter of personal taste, I strongly suggest that human figures not be used unless there is some unavoidably compelling reason for doing so.

TINCTURES

With a few minor exceptions, to a heraldic artist *Azure* is any shade of blue and *Gules* is any shade of red. The basic Rule of Tincture applies to the generally accepted practice of not placing color on color or metal on metal. It does not apply to small details, such as the hoofs, horns, tongues, claws, etc. of animals, and it may be broken for reasons of taste and aesthetics, although such violations rarely work and it is unusual to find them in existing heraldry.

When a blazon calls for *Or,* the color can be shown as gold or yellow, but not both. The same holds true for *Argent,* which may be rendered as silver or white. The exception, as noted in the preceding chapter, is in Spanish coats of arms.

If you are hard-pressed to find pictorial symbols for your coat of arms, you may want to revert to some of the historical associations of colors with attributes. Gold, for example, is associated with nobility, the sun, and, by extension, Sunday. Silver has been connected with justice, purity, and hope. It also represents the moon and Monday. Red is associated with fire, Mars, virility, and Wednesday; blue represents sincerity, piety, and Tuesday; green, of course, represents springtime, humor, and Thursday. (This color did not become popular until the fifteenth century, and it has been suggested that this was because pale green symbolized death. It is recommended that if you want green in your coat of arms, you make sure that the artist uses a strong and vigorous tint.) Black, be-

FIG. 13. Arms of Sir Ian Orr-Ewing, showing electron paths around a nucleus.

FIG. 14. Arms of Lord Penney, atomic scientist, with two representations of electrons.

cause of its basic humility, is associated with religious symbolism. It also represents winter and Friday and is essentially without many cheerful associations in early heraldry. "One might wonder," comments Dennys, "why anyone ever bore black in their arms . . . but fortunately the Middle Ages had a flexible approach to the problems of heraldry."[39] (See Chapter 3 for other color-related symbolism.)

HELMET

Despite its basically militaristic origins, contemporary heraldry, with the exception of those achievements that have warlike charges, are essentially non-military, and the helmet remains as the only military object. (It may be argued that the shield also has military origins; it is, however, now generally accepted as an artistic and aesthetic form which has been used by so many people in such a wide variety of ways that it no longer carries its warlike associations.) Many armigers have simply abandoned the use of the helmet in their arms. If, for purposes of tradition or aesthetics, you prefer to keep the helmet as part of your achievement, the most acceptable is the so-called Esquire's helmet, as shown in the pattern in Chapter 14.

MANTLING

The manner in which the mantling is drawn is as varied as the shield. Contemporary artists tend to keep it fairly simple. The coloring of the mantling is essentially open to personal choice, but traditionally, the mantling tends to consist of the main color and the main metal of the shield. (It is a style I personally favor simply because that I like the way it looks.) If your mantling is to consist of other colors or tinctures, it must be so stated in the blazon.

In place of the mantle you may want to use an ecclesiastical cloak or robe. This is both commonplace and proper when the armiger holds a church office, and of course, the garment that is depicted should be the one that is appropriate to that particular office. Perhaps the strongest argument against such use, however, is that unless one's offspring follow in their ancestor's footsteps, the inclusion of such a cloak in the arms they inherit could prove something of an embarrassment.

MOTTOES

The motto is not an integral part of the coat of arms. In England it is not included in the wording of grants of arms these days. (In Scotland, however, it is customary to include the motto in the grant.) It is entirely possible and proper for more than one person to have the same motto at the same time. Conversely, the motto can be changed freely. It can be in any language, although Latin, English, and French seem to be the most popular. A motto in the language of the country of origin is an excellent way of strengthening the ties that bind.

TORSE

To review: The torse is a wreath consisting of a representation of twisted scarves, generally of the same two tinctures as the mantle, and is shown holding the mantle to the helmet.

AUGMENTATIONS

An augmentation is an addition to a coat of arms granted by a heraldic authority. It may consist of charges added to the arms, a crest or two, supporters, and even a whole new coat of arms to be marshalled with the original coat. In times gone by, there were two reasons for the granting of augmentations: "grace" and "merit." Augmentations of grace were granted to those who, for reasons of political expediency or loyalty, or personality, found grace in the eyes of the sovereign. A grant of merit was made when the monarch felt that some particular act or achievement was worth commemorating through perpetuation in the family coat of arms.

Because of this background of augmentations, it could be considered presumptuous for someone to assume a coat of arms that includes anything resembling an unearned augmentation. Nevertheless, it is (in my opinion) entirely proper to represent, by means of any of the traditional forms of augmentation, a great event or accomplishment, either in the life of the new armiger or one of his or her ancestors. If you decide to include augmentations in your coat of arms, please keep it simple.

CRESTS

If your coat of arms is to include a crest, you will have to decide whether it is to be placed (as is usually the case) atop a helmet, in which case it ought to be something that makes sense in that position. A plume, an arrow, a star, a crescent, a tool or weapon, the figure of an animal, animal horns, and even human figures or arms and legs all could conceivably be affixed to the top of the helmet. On the other hand, a boat riding the ocean waves presents both a practical and an aesthetic challenge.

If the helmet is excluded, then the crest can consist of virtually anything that is heraldically acceptable. The torse, with the crest rising out of it, can be placed directly on top of the shield, or the torse and crest can hover in the air, a practice heraldic purists frown on but which often looks just fine.

SUPPORTERS

Although some countries have no particular rules concerning supporters, in general they are considered augmentations. If you decide to include supporters, remember that they need *a compartment* to stand on, and that it should be appropriate to the supporters. An animal should be standing, perhaps, on a grassy plain or desert sand. A water fowl should probably be standing on a marsh.

THE ULTIMATE ACHIEVEMENT

The basic coat of arms consists of the shield and its charges. The more complicated the achievement becomes, the more difficult it is to maintain a degree of elegance and aesthetic appeal. It is by no means mandatory to include helmet, mantling, torse, crest, supporters, or motto. Each addition to the shield should be in keeping with the basic design so that none of the elements of the entire achievement clash or jar.

MARSHALLING

You may decide to marshall—that is, combine—two coats of arms into one. (For the various techniques of marshalling, see

Chapter 3.) There is, as you now know, a long and detailed set of procedures under which the arms of husbands and wives may be marshalled, and then later separated, all based primarily on the rules concerning the inheritance of arms by women. Inasmuch as we have already denied the concept that women may not inherit arms, we may as well deny the strictures by which arms may be combined and then separated. If, therefore, you and your spouse plan to marshall your arms, it is recommended that you do so with the understanding that these new arms will be passed on to your children.

When an official wants to include some aspect of the coat of arms or some other heraldry-like symbol of a state, city, nation, military service, church, or even a corporation, he or she is, in effect, marshalling arms.

Marshalling—or a variation of it—may be a method of recovering some benefit from an unfortunate circumstance. You have perhaps already purchased (or may have access to) one of the commercially offered coats of arms "for your family name" but are reluctant to use it because you are not convinced that you have a hereditary right to do so. You could possibly include one of the charges from such a coat of arms in your new design. If, for example, your name is Howard, a heraldry merchant may have sold you the augmented arms of Thomas Howard, Earl of Surrey, granted in the sixteenth century and including a demi-lion, fleurs-de-lis, and *cross-crosslets fitchy*. (A *crosslet* is a cross whose members are again crossed near the ends; *fitchy* refers to a cross that tapers to a point at the bottom.) One of these charges can find a comfortable home in your new coat of arms.

Take your time in designing your achievement. Give some consideration to each of the elements to be included and their symbolism. The coat of arms is a pictorial representation of you and your family. It is intensely personal, symbolizing not only your life and your interests, but your taste. Give it lasting meaning so that your children will enjoy displaying it when they inherit it.

Most of all, it is hoped that putting together a coat of arms will be fun for its own sake, and ultimately rewarding. After all, it is not called "an achievement" for nothing.

8

Registering Your Coat of Arms

Earlier, I mentioned that I had purchased a coat of arms for my "family name" from Halbert's, of Bath, Ohio, and had subsequently lost it to an editor to whom it was sent for possible use as an illustration. For this book, I decided to obtain another copy of this coat of arms and wrote to Halbert's, inquiring as to its availability. I was dismayed to receive the following form letter in reply:

Dear Friend:

After ten years of selling "Coats-of-Arms" and surname research reports, Halbert's, Inc., is suspending its heraldic operations. Therefore, we will not be able to process your recent inquiry.

As you may know, Halbert's has expanded into other areas of business—mainly art and collectibles. While the heraldic business has declined over the past few years, these other areas have been expanding rapidly and now require 100% of our attention.

Over the next six months* we will be evaluating this decision, and should we change our minds and resume the selling of heraldic products, we will be sure to notify you.

Again, thank you for your inquiry, and we are sorry we are unable to fulfill your order.

* The letter is signed with the initials "MDH" and is undated. (The envelope was postmarked February 29, 1980.)

At the same time, I sent a postcard to the other colossus of heraldic merchandising, the Sanson Institute of Heraldry in Boston. The card was returned, stamped: "Addressee Unknown."

So now we are faced with a problem that comes from dealing with heraldry merchants, and that has nothing to do with ethics or aesthetics. Even if we accept their offerings, particularly those that have been specially designed for us, allegedly based on historical data, there is, for all practical purposes, no readily available permanent record of those arms. The recording of a coat of arms supplied by a heraldry merchant appears to depend upon the exigencies and vagaries of the marketplace.

The fact that Halbert's has gone into a more lucrative field and that Sanson has apparently disappeared does not eliminate the problem by any means: There are still a number of heraldry merchants offering their wares. Should you purchase a coat of arms from any of them, and should they then decide, for whatever reason, to retire from the heraldry business, where can you or anyone else go for records and confirmations?

There are two important reasons for recording your coat of arms. The first has already been alluded to—the need for a permanent record somewhere for future reference. The second reason is that it may prove useful or necessary at some point to demonstrate that you are the proud possessor of a particular coat of arms.

There is a third reason; admittedly, it is more philosophical than practical. It is in the best tradition of heraldry that a coat of arms be recorded. It seems to me that the entire process of designing a coat of arms is incomplete unless that design is made part of a permanent record somewhere. There are several ways of doing so.

The New England Historical and Genealogical Society will record the assumed arms of any American. If you write to their Committee on Heraldry at 101 Newberry Street, Boston, MA 02116 and request it, they will send you an application form for such recording. The completed form is returned with a relatively low recording fee, and in due course the secretary of the committee will return the form to you confirming that your coat of arms has indeed been recorded.

If you want to accomplish both the recording and the protection of your arms, your best recourse is probably the U.S. copyright laws.

On January 1, 1978, a new and much-needed copyright statute came into effect in this country. In an address before the American Society of Journalists and Authors, the distinguished literary attorney, Harriet Pilpel, referred to this new law as "the attorneys' fair employment practices act," alluding to its complexities. For the new armiger, however, copyrighting a coat of arms is a fairly simple matter. Write to the Copyright Office, Library of Congress, Washington, D.C. 20059 and ask for "Application for Copyright Registration" forms TX and VA. Form TX is for the registration of a non-dramatic literary work, and this is the form to be used for registering the blazon. It is relatively easy to complete and comes with a full set of instructions.

For the title of the work, say "Blazon of Coat of Arms of (fill in your name)." For the name of the author, give your own name and nationality or place of residence ("domicile"). As for the rest of the form, you need only complete the boxes dealing with reproduction for use of blind or physically handicapped persons, correspondence, certification, and mailing address. The completed form, with a check for $10 made payable to Register of Copyrights, should be sent to the Register of Copyrights at the Library of Congress. Once you have accomplished this registration, your coat of arms is, for all practical purposes, effectively recorded and, to some extent, protected against use by others.

Problems may arise from the fact that a blazon can be rendered in several ways, depending upon its interpretation by the artist. You may, therefore, also want to submit Form VA, which is an application for the copyright registration of a work of the visual arts. This will protect the visual representation of your coat of arms. Form VA is very similar to Form TX, and it too requires a payment of $10. With Form TX you will be expected to include a copy of the blazon; Form VA requires the inclusion of the pictorial representation. And, of course, you should retain copies of the completed forms for your own records.

Under the new law, "the basic copyright term will be the life of the author and fifty years after the author's death."

If you can prove English ancestry, you may be able to obtain a grant of arms from the College of Arms. They may even supply a grant for the arms which you have devised (assuming they are heraldically acceptable), making only some small change to indicate that they have had a hand in it. The cost can be high, easily exceeding a thousand dollars. (In addition, you may wind up having to pay a genealogist to prove your ancestry.) Such grants are called "honorary arms." If you are interested, write to: Secretary to the Earl Marshal, The College of Arms, Queen Victoria Street, London, EC4V 4BT, England.

If you have a Scottish ancestor who was armigerous, you can request a grant of his arms from the Scottish heraldic authorities. If you can prove Scottish descent from a non-armigerous ancestor, you must request a grant of arms *for your ancestor*. You may then request that the arms be reassigned to you. Information can be obtained by writing to the Lord Lyon, Lyon Office, H.M. New Register House, Edinburgh, EH1 3YT, Scotland.

If you are of Spanish descent or, oddly enough, live in a state or territory that was once a Spanish colony, you may be able to obtain a grant of arms from Spain. There are a number of conditions involved and they tend to be somewhat complex. For details write to Cronista Rey De Armas, Calle de Atocha, 91, Madrid, Spain.

Most other countries have heraldic organizations, most of which exercise little or no actual authority. These will be found in Chapter 13.

Several attempts have been made to establish heraldic colleges in the United States, but most of these have proven to be abortive. At this writing, there exists the American College of Heraldry, Box 19347, New Orleans, LA 70179, which "grants" and registers coats of arms. The permanency of its records is, I suspect, closely connected with its success and survival.

9

The Uses of Heraldry

The opportunities for displaying a coat of arms are virtually limitless. Where it is proper and where it is considered ostentatious is something else again. To some extent, we are confronted with the same problem that presented itself at the beginning of Chapter 7: the question of aesthetics and good taste.

Almost since heraldry's early beginnings, it has been customary to display a full achievement, either as a painting or as a stone carving, above the entrance to a castle. In view of the fact that so few of us live in castles these days, it is entirely appropriate to display one's arms over the door to one's home. There are many other acceptable, and indeed desirable, ways of using an armorial achievement for purposes of decoration and identification, and some of these will be discussed shortly. But even here there seem to be very fine lines of distinction, some of which are, frankly, a mystery to me. For example, it is considered good form to wear one's coat of arms on certain articles of clothing, such as the breast pocket of a blazer. It is unclear, therefore, why those who consider themselves experts in the tasteful applications of heraldry deplore its use on beach towels and bathrobes. Neubecker suggests that "because arms are ensigns of honor, the tendency has been to use them in the adornment of personal treasures . . ."[40] but one person's treasure may be another person's trash. Ultimately, then, one's own sense of aesthetics and personal taste must prevail.

One of the most common uses of heraldry is in the form of armorial bookplates. It is a tradition that dates back to antiquity; most of the books produced in the Middle Ages were lavishly decorated with heraldic devices. Prayer books and other religious works were often decorated with coats of arms on their covers, and books containing wills were frequently identified by the coats of arms.

A cleanly designed coat of arms can be effectively rendered in black and white for a bookplate, using the appropriate hatches. (See Figure 10.) The achievement will have to be reproduced on a plate, the initial cost of which can be fairly high. It should be considered an investment, however, because these plates last a very long time and can be used repeatedly. Bookplates can be obtained from most engravers and fine printers. For a company that specializes in this product at reasonable prices, write to the Antioch Bookplate Company, Yellowsprings, OH 45387. Incidentally, it may be wise to break another heraldic tradition when ordering bookplates. Customarily, the family name does not appear with the coat of arms; it is considered a redundancy. Perhaps an exception should be made with bookplates to prod the consciences of those who borrow books and are slow to return them.

Another long-standing tradition is the display of heraldry on coaches and carriages. Since these have mostly gone the way of castles, it is entirely proper and, again, rather attractive to place your coat of arms or a version of it on your car or boat. If you are in fact a boat owner, you may want to have a flag or pennant that either reproduces your coat of arms or uses it as the basis for a design, to be flown proudly from your craft.

Armorial jewelry is most attractive. Pendants, cuff links, and brooches are especially good-looking. A signet ring with the coat of arms is also a handsome addition to a collection of potential family heirlooms. (It should, of course, be deeply engraved and in reverse, if it is to serve properly as a seal.) A good source of heraldic jewelry is Heraldica Imports, Inc., 21 West 46th Street, New York, NY 10036. As one of their advertisements correctly claims, this is "the most exclusive and personal jewelry there is . . . a limited edition of one!"

Arms can be used to decorate virtually any household object. Traditionally, they have been used on silver, porcelain, and glass tableware. Such artifacts are very expensive but they do have enormous potential as family heirlooms.

Personal stationery bearing a coat of arms is both elegant and beautiful. One of the most effective types incorporates "blind embossing," in which the coat of arms is embossed without ink. This is particularly effective on invitations. It must be remembered, however, that blind embossing can look simply awful with a complicated coat of arms unless it is done with great care.

A variation on the use of the coat of arms is a badge. Badges of all sorts have become so much a part of contemporary American culture that we tend to take them for granted, and most of us are totally unaware of the fact that almost all badges now in existence are heraldic either in origin or in their design. In many major cities, police officers' badges are referred to as "shields," despite the fact that, with the exception of the occasional lucky accident in which they deflect a bullet or a blade, these badges shield precious little. Most people at some point in their lives wear something closely resembling a badge, usually as a symbol of authority or occupation or to indicate membership in some organization. Collegians are not likely to think of their fraternity or sorority pins as badges, but, in fact, they are.

Badges, which often consist of either the crest or one of the main charges of a coat of arms, encircled by a wreath, can be used whenever a more simple heraldic design is preferable or when the coat of arms is too large or complicated for some particular object.

CIVIC ARMS

The use of some sort of symbol or totem around which communities and tribes rallied probably goes back to prehistory. "At the dawn of heraldry the tendency to have such symbols became standardized in the use of public arms by communities as such."[41] In Western Europe it is practically impossible to find a village, town, city, or province that does not have its own coat of arms. In this country each of the fifty states has a state seal, many of which adhere closely to traditional heraldic design. The flags of Delaware, Connecticut, Missouri, Maine, Illinois, Michigan, Oregon, Pennsylvania, New York, New Jersey, Utah, Vermont, and Wisconsin all carry state emblems featuring heraldic shields. Most of them have crests, supporters, and mottoes. Many major cities also have heraldry-like emblems which can be found on everything from the mayor's official limousine to the gates of the city dump. In other words, there is ample precedent for your city or town designing and using a coat of arms if it does not already have one.

Furthermore, there are a number of valid reasons for doing so, not the least of which is the purely aesthetic: Just as an individual coat of arms is worth having for its own sake, so is a municipal or community coat of arms. It provides the community with a means of identity, a spirit of unity, and a sense of historical continuity.

To be sure, there are practical aspects as well: An official coat of arms offers rapid and ready identification of official documents, signs, proclamations, and buildings and vehicles. (It can be carried to excess. A couple of years ago, I participated in a "press tour" of a major southern city whose business leaders were engaged in a major campaign to improve their community's seriously tarnished image—the result of a series of unsavory political and sociological events. Among the dignitaries presented to me was a councilman on whom most of the stereotypes of small-time southern politicians seemed to be based. He had a clear and active dislike for New Yorkers, which he did not hesitate to articulate. Nevertheless, apparently out of some sense of public duty, he muttered, somewhat halfheartedly, that if he could be of any assistance to me, I should feel free to call upon him. He presented me with two business cards. One represented his automobile dealership; the other was his official city council card on which was emblazoned the civic coat of arms—entirely in gold and quite illegible. Its overall appearance was about as genuine as the councilman's offer of assistance, which, mercifully, I have so far managed to do without.)

The benefits of a community coat of arms are considerable when compared to the cost involved—unless your local politicians resort to such favorite ploys as establishing a committee, hiring consultants, and paying patronage to some local artist. A municipal coat of arms can be devised with the same care and simplicity as is recommended for a personal achievement. There is no need to junk all the official signs and stationery once the coat of arms has been rendered. The design can simply be incorporated in these items as new supplies are ordered.

The same factors that go into the making of a personal coat of arms should serve as the basis for civic arms. Perhaps the city is named after a foreign place, in which case some element of the original namesake's arms could be adopted. The founder of the community may have been armigerous and his coat of arms could also serve as a basis of civic arms. Perhaps the name could be interpreted in canting arms. Even the locale's major attraction or chief industry could be included.

An excellent example of a community coat of arms that incorporates most of these elements is the arms of the English town of Wallsend. The arms show an eagle standing on top of a wall and surrounded with golden drops. The wall represents Hadrian's Wall, at the eastern end of which the town is situated. The eagle represents the ancient Romans, who built the wall. The gold drops signify the local copper-smelting industry, and the black background represents the regional coal industry. (The blazon is *Sable, goutted Or, in base an embattled wall; thereon an eagle with wings displayed both Or.*)

BUSINESS HERALDRY

Heraldry proliferates almost as much in the world of commerce as it does in government. While purveyors of automobiles, cigarettes, and beer seem to be especially fond of decorated shields—some of which are execrable heraldry—they by no means have a corner on the market.

There is a long-standing tradition in other countries for businesses to have their own coats of arms, and this applies to small one- or two-owner companies as well as to large multinational corporations.

Designers of business heraldry should keep in mind that it is not necessary to stay with the traditional charges normally associated with personal or even municipal heraldry. Symbols from mathematics, chemistry, physics, electricity, architecture, medicine, engineering, and almost any other field that has its own set of symbols are all applicable to business heraldry. The major factors to consider are, as always, aesthetics and appropriateness.

For many industries, endurance should also be a consideration. With rapidly advancing technology, particularly in the fields of electronics, data processing, and communications, care should be taken to avoid designing a coat of arms that will "date" the enterprise. A travel agency, for example, that includes an airplane propeller in its coat of arms is not likely to be viewed as an up-to-date company. On the other hand, some very old symbols, such as a sailing vessel, are entirely appropriate because they suggest tradition and stability.

Commercial heraldry can be used in exactly the same ways as personal heraldry—on stationery, badges, official company vehicles, handbooks, and, as a particularly nice touch, on premiums for employees and customers, especially nicely made jewelry.

INSTITUTIONAL HERALDRY

I wonder if there exists anywhere in this country a society, fraternal order, social welfare agency, charity, or school that does not have some kind of emblem. Chances are that most of those emblems, or "logos," if not actually heraldic, are readily adaptable to heraldic design. What has been said about civic and corporate heraldry applies as well to institutional heraldry. Virtually any kind of organization or institution can and should use a coat of arms. All sorts of professional and trade organizations, including trade unions, have them; it is a tradition that dates back almost to the origins of heraldry itself, and some of the most ancient and honorable arms of Europe and England include black diamond shapes (for coal), picks, spades, railway locomotives, airplanes, padlocks, etc. The Grocers' Company of London has cloves in its coat of arms; the Fishmongers' Company has a trio of dolphins and another of pike, and the Auctioneers' and Estate Agents' Institute has an auctioneer's hammer in its achievement.

(One note of caution: educational institutions have used the Lamp of Learning and books in coats of arms to the point where these have almost become heraldic clichés.)

The English College of Arms is empowered to devise arms for American corporate bodies. This includes towns (provided that the consent of the governor of the state is given first) as well as other corporations such as business enterprises, schools, organizations, etc. The College of Arms will design the coat of arms and then record it. Then, a far as the College is concerned, those arms can never again be granted. (Nevertheless, it is probably wise to have them copyrighted. Businesses may further want to register their arms as a trademark with the U. S. Patent and Trademark Office.)

I have always felt that one of the more appealing aspects of "impersonal" arms is that they can be freely displayed by anyone with even the remotest connection to their sources of origin. Among my growing collection of cuff links is a set consisting of the arms of London, and another with the arms of Amsterdam, two of my favorite cities. I am also the proud possessor of a denim windbreaker, the back of which is decorated with about a dozen patches, each representing a country I have visited, and primarily heraldic in design. There are some who consider such a display as ostentatious. Let them; I do not care.

In heraldry, as in food, art, and music, the principle of *chacun à son goût* ("each to his own taste") seems to prevail.

10

Heraldry as a Hobby

Many years ago, I discovered the joys of being a "building watcher," a diversion which, happily, my wife shares. It is an activity that is not without certain hazards, particularly in major urban areas where pedestrian and vehicular traffic are likely to be both abundant and fast-moving. Still, a dedicated building watcher soon learns to enjoy the architectural delights that abound while avoiding embarrassing and even dangerous collisions with cars and people.

In New York City, there are hundreds of buildings that are profusely decorated in fascinating ways—most of them dating back to the early 1920s and before. A brownstone house in our neighborhood has two portrait medallions. One is obviously that of President Franklin D. Roosevelt; the other appears to be of Sigmund Freud. (We have no idea why they are there; we speculate that at one time the building must have housed something like the WPA Psychiatric Institute.) We are amazed at the number of people who pass that building repeatedly and never notice the medallions. Nor have they ever seen the race between the tortoise and the hare that goes on in perpetuity along a cornice above the third story of a huge apartment house located at a major Manhattan intersection.

All manner of beasts, birds, fish, and fowl—not to mention people—and ranging from the beautiful to the bizarre, grace these buildings. And more often than not, they appear in the form of a coat of arms or what someone concluded, either through ignorance or questionable taste, a coat of arms ought to look like.

Unfortunately, with the zeal that characterizes all reformers, urban developers—both public and private—are tearing many of these buildings down and replacing them with steel, concrete and glass boxes that are virtually devoid of any character. If, therefore, you want to study architectural heraldry just for the pleasure of doing so, you had best start soon. The other rewarding treasures you are bound to find are dividends well worth the minimal effort. But, remember: When you are building-watching, try to watch where you are going. It is an activity recommended for pedestrians and passengers only.

Heraldry can be found all over the place: at airports, in supermarkets, in automobile showrooms. Among the best places to look for it are churches, especially Roman Catholic and Episcopal. Nowhere does heraldry abound as it does in the churches and cathedrals of Europe. Even modern churches are likely to have banners, plaques, and artifacts that are heraldic, but the old churches are the best. Many church pews and boxes have over them a plaque or banner with the achievement of the family, who, for centuries, have worshipped in that spot. You are probably familiar with the brass rubbings taken from church tombs of knights and their ladies. Invariably these tombs depict the deceased lying at peace, with his head pillowed on his helmet, his feet resting on some small animal, and near his breast a shield bearing his coat of arms.

Examining antique religious books is also a most satisfying pastime for those who not only want to see a wide variety of beautiful heraldry but who enjoy fine examples of the bookmaking art. There are in most libraries—and many bookstores—facsimile editions of Books of Hours and other carefully and meticulously hand-illuminated religious treatises. I have yet to see one that does not include some fine heraldry. (I have also seen some that include what can only be described as outrageous heraldry.)

These are, of course, passive pastimes. If you would prefer a more active involvement in the pleasures of heraldry, your choices are many. There are collectors who accumulate all sorts of heraldic artifacts: tableware, jewelry, plaques, etc. I know one couple who acquire a souvenir demitasse spoon whenever they visit a city or country for the first time. Invariably, they select one that has a heraldic design at the end of the handle. This is a working collection; parts of it are likely to show up on their dinner table when they entertain. Because the arms are so many and of such varied design, they can never be mistaken as the couple's own. Such display is, therefore, entirely acceptable.

Some collectors specialize in heraldic bookplates; others limit themselves to acquiring heraldic postage stamps. This may seem a rather dull pastime, best suited to the sedentary, solitary, introvert of limited interests. But one look at the overwhelming beauty, variety, geography, history, and linguistic delights of a page of properly mounted heraldic stamps quickly dispels that notion.

As you now know something about the origins, traditions, and uses of heraldry, you may want to make yourself available as an amateur consultant for your friends, relatives, and the various organizations and institutions with which you are involved. Again, the rewards of such a hobby can be enormous. Some may regard heraldry as a somewhat dry, even pedantic, field. But you now know that this is not at all the case. If you actively participate in the heraldic interests of others, you will find yourself deeply involved not only in the obvious fields of graphic design and genealogy, but in history, geography, zoology, mythology, religion, and even linguistics and etymology. There are few other pastimes that can offer such a wide range of fascinating fields. (I might mention—although with a modicum of trepidation—a variation on this theme: the designing of deliberately bogus, even comic coats of arms for relatives and friends. The trepidation arises from the possibility that someone, somewhere, someday, might take such arms seriously.)

If you would like to pursue an interest in heraldry with some seriousness, you might consider becoming a member of the Heraldry Society. Although it is a British organization, its members are far-flung, as are its heraldic interests. For information, write to the society's secretary at 28 Museum Street, London WC1A ILH, England. The society offers, in addition to a magazine and newsletter, a series of courses and examinations through which you can become a full-fledged heraldist.

But the sheer enjoyment of heraldry requires little effort or dedi-

cation. You need only an eye for it. An interesting coat of arms,
whether ugly or beautiful, can inspire musings and speculations to
satisfy the imagination of anyone who, no matter how demanding
his or her particular rat-race may be, still has a trace of romance in
his or her soul.

11

A Heraldic Glossary

This Glossary serves two purposes. First, it is intended as a ready and easy reference of heraldic terms and their pronunciation. Second, it is a relatively painless method of becoming familiar with most of the more commonly used heraldic terminology. It is highly recommended that you read through the entire Glossary at least once or twice, if for no other reason than to have some indication of all of the various design options available to you when devising your own coat of arms. Many of the charges defined in the Glossary are depicted in Figure 32 and elsewhere throughout the book.

Regrettably, this Glossary is by no means complete. A comprehensive heraldic dictionary would require a volume all of its own. (This has, in fact, been produced by the estimable Richmond Herald of Arms, J. P. Brooke-Little, in his highly recommended book, *An Heraldic Alphabet;* see Bibliography.)

The language of heraldry offers a frequently frustrating challenge to those who pride themselves on being careful spellers. Heraldry originated and developed during a time when the English language was undergoing changes. Although English is basically a Germanic tongue (i.e., Anglo-Saxon), with the Norman conquest of England many words of Latin origin were introduced into the language by way of Norman French—which was also undergoing changes. The result is a linguistic salad, seasoned by a rather carefree attitude toward spelling at a time when literacy was low and those who could write tended to spell words approximately the way they sounded. In heraldry, words that were once French tended to be anglicized. *Affronté,* for example, while certainly correct in usage, has mostly given way to *affronty.*

Uncertain spelling and linguistic mixture inevitably give rise to problems of pronunciation. Throughout the Glossary, possible pronunciations of some of the more difficult words are offered. They are not necessarily the only correct ones. If formerly French spellings can be anglicized, why not formerly French pronunciations as well? Thus, the first syllable of *cinquefoil* can be pronounced *SANK* (French) or *SINK* (English).

By and large, words can be pronounced as they are spelled. If an obviously French word offends you when pronounced as though it were English, then by all means use the French pronunciation. For example, *Chambers Twentieth Century Dictionary* (Edinburgh; W. and R. Chambers, Ltd., 1972) gives the pronunciation for *couchant* as "KOWCH-ant." Following the rule of pronouncing words as they are spelled and as though they were English, this is perfectly acceptable. But I think it sounds awkward; I prefer—and have so indicated—the pronunciation koo-SHAHNT.

As I said, *chacun à son goût.*

(*NOTE: Italicized words* in the definitions are defined elsewhere in the Glossary.)

ABASED, ABAISED, ABAISSÉ: Used to describe a *charge* that is placed somewhat lower in the *achievement* than it normally would be.

ABATEMENT: Applies to a *charge* variously defined as "a difference for illegitimacy" and "a mark of dishonor" added to the *achievement.* It is apparently more evident in fiction than in life. See *stains* and Index.

ABOUTÉ: Positioned end to end.

ACCESSORIES: All of the appurtenances of a heraldic *achievement,* excluding the *shield.*

ACCOLLÉ: Describes two *shields* placed alongside each other and touching. Also, sometimes a synonym for *gorged.*

ACCOMPANIED, ACCOMPAGNÉ: A synonym for "between."

ACHIEVEMENT: The complete armorial display—the *shield,* the *crest,* the *mantle,* etc. See Index.

ADDORSED, ENDORSED, INDORSED, ADOSSÉ: Back-to-back, to describe the position of animals, birds, etc.

ADUMBRATED (a-DUM-brated), ADUMBRATION (AH-dum-BRAY-shun) : Describes a *charge* shown only in outline form or, if in the same *tincture* as the *field,* to create the impression of relief.

AESCULAPIUS (ES-kyoo-LAY-pee-us), ROD OF: The familiar rod with a serpent wound around it that is the emblem of physicians and other professions and institutions involved in health care. Aesculapius was the Roman god of healing and medicine. See *Caduceus.*

AFFRONTY (a-FRONT-ee), AFFRONTÉ: An animal or other *charge* placed on the *shield* so that it is seen displaying its full front view to the observer.

AGNUS DEI (AG-nus DAY): The Holy Lamb. This *charge* is always depicted as a lamb *passant* with a halo around its head. Often its *dexter* foreleg holds a staff topped with a cross and from which a white *pennon* bearing a red cross flows. Also *blazoned* as "paschal lamb."

ALAN, ALAND, ALANT, ALUNT: A short-eared mastiff.

ALERION, ALLERION: An *eagle,* usually shown without its beak or legs, which may explain why it is no longer very popular.

ALISÉ (alice-AY): Rounded, as the ends of some *crosses.*

ALLUMÉ (a-loo-MAY): Describing a beast's eyes dotted with color.

ALTAR: A square or rectangular pedestal almost always with a flame on top of it.

AMPHISBAENA (AM-fis-BEE-na): A *serpent* with a head at each end of its body.

AMPHISIEN COCKATRICE: See *basilisk.*

ANCHOR: Typically depicted upright with a ring at the top. An anchor with a rope twisted around its shank is *blazoned* "an anchor cabled" or "a foul anchor." See also *stock* and *fluke.*

ANCHORED, ANCHORY, ANCRÉ: A "cross anchored" has each of its limbs ending in an anchor's *flukes,* i.e., the points or barbs of an anchor.

ANIMÉ: See *incensed.*

ANKH: A kind of Egyptian "cross," except that the area above the horizontal crossbeam is a *voided* ellipse. It is an ancient symbol for energy and life.

ANNULET (ANN-yuh-lit): A ring; in British heraldry it is the *mark of difference* for the fifth son.

ANNULETTY (ANN-yuh-LET-ee) ANNULATED, ANNULY: Having rings at the ends.

ANTELOPE: In heraldry, the antelope has the body of the real thing, but the face of a heraldic *tyger,* tusks, serrated horns, tufts down its back, and the tail of a *lion.* To avoid confusion, antelopes should be *blazoned* either "heraldic antelope," or if the realistic version is preferred, "an antelope *proper.*"

ANVIL: The blacksmith's mainstay, shown as it exists in real life.

APAUMÉ (AH-po-MAY), APAUMY, APPAUMÉ, APPALMED: Describing a *gauntlet* or *hand* with the palm showing.

ARBALEST, ARBLAST: A *crossbow.*

ARCHED, ARCHY, ENARCHED: Shaped like an arch; often used to describe a *chief, fess,* or *chevron.*

ARGENT (AR-jint): Silver or white; often abbreviated arg., ar., or a. See Index.

ARM: The human appendage. The *blazon* should always indicate whether the arm is *sinister* or *dexter.*

ARMED: When used to describe human figures or parts thereof, "armed" means wearing armor. More typically, it refers to the "arms" of animals: beaks, horns, claws, tusks, etc. when these are of a different color from the rest of the beast's body.

ARMIGER (AR-mij-er): A person who bears *arms.*

ARMIGEROUS (ar-MIJ-erus): *Arms*-bearing.

ARMILLARY SPHERE: A medieval model of the heavens. The British spell it "armilliary," with the accent on the second syllable.

ARMORIAL BEARINGS: A heraldic *achievement.*

ARMS: Strictly speaking, this term applies only to the *shield* and its *charges,* but it is often used to refer to the entire *achievement.*

ARROW: As a *charge,* arrows may be shown singly or in bundles. If the feathers and points are of a *tincture* that differs from the shaft, it should be so *blazoned*—"flighted" for the feathers and *barbed* for the head (sometimes described as "feathered and armed"). The *blazon* should also specify the position of the arrow.

ASSURGENT (a-SURJ-int): Arising from; generally referring to creatures rising out of the ocean.

AT GAZE: A synonym for *statant guardant,* used to describe members of the *deer* family.

ATTIRES: A synonym for the antlers of the *deer* family. The adjectival form is "attired," which is also sometimes used in connection with the costume of a human figure, but in such cases *vested* or *habited* are more common.

AUGMENTATION: See Index and Figure 15.

FIG. 15.
Augmentation
(with inescutcheon)

AZURE (AZH-yoor) : Blue. Typically, this is abbreviated as b. (One would assume that az. would be more common, but, ever the practical practitioners, heraldists held that az. is easily confused with ar. See Index.

BADGE: An identifying device based on a coat of *arms*. See Index.

BADGER: The animal; useful for its characteristics and in *canting* arms; usually *blazoned* "brock."

BAGWYN: A mythical beast that resembles a heraldic *antelope* except that it has the body and tail of a *horse*.

BALANCE: A pair of scales. As a *charge,* commonly used by those who claim to practice law, but it is by no means their exclusive property and may be used by anyone whose business or profession involves the weighing of facts, philosophies, or substances.

BANDED: Encircled by a band; often used to describe a sheaf of wheat (see *garb*) or of *arrows* when the band is of another color.

BAR: See Index.

BAR GEMEL (JEM-mil) : Two horizontal narrow *bars* placed close together, somewhat like railroad tracks.

BARB: A sepal, the leaf-like object between the petals of the heraldic *rose*.

BARBED: Having *barbs,* also, having a human beard; also, having the head of an *arrow* or a *spear.*

BARNACLE: A rather unpleasant-looking instrument used in a *horse's* nose. It is horseshoe-shaped and has *barbs* on the inside. It is also known as a "brey" or "horse brey." The term also sometimes refers to the barnacle goose. In heraldry, it never refers to the crustacean that clings to the bottoms of vessels.

BARRY: Divided into an even number of horizontal bars; the number may be specified. Sometimes *blazoned* "barruly." See Figure 5.

BARRY-BENDY: Divided *barry* and *bendy,* giving a kind of angular checkerboard effect. See *bend, bendy.*

BARRY-PILY: Divided horizontally into *pile*-shaped segments, the number of which may or may not be specified. See *pile, pily.*

BAR SINISTER: A mark of bastardy. See *baton.*

BARWISE: Designating that the *charges* are to be placed on the *field* horizontally.

BASE: The bottom portion of the *shield.* See Figures 2 and 4.

BASILISK: A mythical creature resembling a *cockatrice* except for the dragonlike head affixed to the end of its tail; sometimes referred to as an "amphisien cockatrice."

BATON: A *bendlet couped* at both ends; that is, a narrow diagonal stripe the ends of which are cut off before reaching the borders of the *shield.* When the baton runs from the *sinister chief* to the *dexter base* it is usually a mark of bastardy, especially among royalty. It is also known as a "baston," which may account for this usage. See Index.

BATTERING RAM: A cylindrical shaft, at one end of which is a *ram's* head. Around the middle are two bands holding rings from which the battering ram can be suspended.

BATTLE AX: Frequently used in ancient heraldry. There seem to be few modern applications for it.

BEACON: A cagelike affair, containing a fire and set on a pole mounted on a tripod, and with a ladder leaning against the pole.

BEAKED: Used when referring to the beaks of birds or mythical beasts.

BEAM: The upright portion of an *anchor;* also called "shank."

BEAR: The animal; see Index.

BEARING: A synonym for a heraldic *charge.*

BEAVER: The animal; typically associated with industry. See *castor.*

BEE: The insect. It is shown *displayed,* but is properly *blazoned volant.*

BEEHIVE: In heraldry, the domelike hive is used and is typically "beset with bees."

BELL: A frequently used *charge.* If the word appears by itself in the *blazon,* it usually refers to a church bell; otherwise the type of bell should be specified.

BELLED: With bells attached, as on an animal or bird, or the cap of a jester.

BEND: One of the *ordinaries;* a wide band that runs from the *dexter chief* of the shield to the *sinister base,* and occupying about a third of the field. See Figure 4.

BENDLET: A narrow version—about half the width—of a *bend.*

BENDWISE: Running in the direction of a *bend.*

BENDY: Divided into an even number of *bendwise* portions. The divisions will always go from *dexter chief* to *sinister base;* if the reverse is desired, the *blazon* should specify *bendy sinister.* The number of divisions may or may not be specified.

BENEDICTION: A *hand apaumé,* with the index and middle fingers upright and the others closed, is said to be "raised in benediction"; popular among the clergy.

BEZANT (BEZ-ant, buh-ZANT): A gold *roundel,* named after a gold coin.

BEZANTY (buh-ZAN-tee): Strewn with *bezants.*

BICORPORATE: Having two bodies.

BILLET: A vertical rectangle.

BILLETY, BILLETÉ (bil-LET-tee): Strewn with *billets.* See Figure 16.

FIG. 16. Billety

BLACKAMOOR, BLACKAMOOR'S HEAD: The figure or head of a black man; sometimes *blazoned* "a Negro's head."

BLASTED: Said of a *tree* that is withered and without leaves.

BLAZON (BLAY-zun): As a noun, the description of a coat of *arms;* as a verb, to describe a coat of arms. See Index.

BLEU CÉLESTE (BLUE suh-LEST): This color, a pale sky-blue, is a relatively recent addition to heraldry, used to show some association with aviation.

BLIGHTED: A synonym for *blasted.*

BLUE BOTTLE: One of the curiosities of heraldic language, this refers not to the fly, but to the blue cornflower.

BLUEMANTLE PURSUIVANT: An English heraldic officer.

BOAR: A popular heraldic *charge,* shown with bristles down its back and with long tusks. The boar's head is also popular, usually shown *erased* or *couped.*

BONACON: A mythical beast resembling a *bull* but with a *horse's* tail and a short mane. Its horns have an inward curl and are therefore useless, so the bonacon repels its attackers by discharging "burning excrement" at them. Perhaps acceptable during the more earthy Middle Ages, it hardly seems an appropriate *charge* these days, except, perhaps, for some rather specialized kinds of symbolism.

BONE: Always shown with a knob at each end, unless some specific type of bone is indicated.

BONNET: The *cap* that is worn inside a *coronet.*

BOOK: Educational institutions and individuals involved in the production of the printed word have made the book an extremely popular *charge.* The *blazon* should state whether the book is to be depicted closed or open and whether it has clasps. See Frontispiece and Index.

BORDURE (BOARD-yoor): A border running around the edge of the *shield.*

BOUGET (boo-GAY): Usually *blazoned* "water-bouget," a stylized version of two leather water bags supported by a yoke; it can be depicted in several ways, although no variation is made in the *blazon.*

BOURDON (BOOR-don): Also known as a "pilgrim's or palmer's staff." (Palmers are pilgrims carrying palm leaves.) It has religious symbolism, but is an excellent *charge* in the *canting arms* of people named Burden, Pilgrim, Palmer, etc. Furthermore, modern dictionaries define "bourdon" as an organ stop and a bagpipe drone, and using the pilgrim's staff in these contexts, while perhaps a little obscure, is nevertheless valid. The staff is shown as a rod with a knob at the upper end, a point at the bottom end, and a kind of coat hook near the top.

Bow: In heraldry, this is always the archer's longbow, which is to be shown bent unless *blazoned* otherwise. The bow is described as "stringed" if the string is of a *tincture* that differs from the bow itself.

BRACED, BRAZED: Interlaced.

BRETESSED, BRETTESSÉ: *Embattled* both top and bottom.

BREY: Synonym for *barnacle.*

BRIDGE: Because there is no particular form to be used as a heraldic *charge,* the type of bridge must be *blazoned* in some detail.

BROCK: Synonym for *badger.*

BUCK: Synonym for *stag.*

BUCKLE: There is no specific heraldic buckle, so the shape—circular, oval, square, rectangular, diamond—should be specified in the *blazon,* as well as its position.

BUGLE HORN: The fairly typical animal's horn that has been adapted for use as a bugle. It is always curved and is often referred to as a "hunting horn" or simply as a "horn."

BULL: The animal. See Index.

BURGEONEE (BUR-jonny): A *fleur-de-lis* with closed petals, giving a budlike appearance.

CABLE: The rope or chain of an *anchor.*

CABOSHED (cuh-BOSH'D), CABOSSED: Describing an animal's head shown *affronty* without any part of the neck being visible. Heraldic *leopards* and *lions* are never caboshed; they are instead *faced.*

CADENCY: The differencing of arms for *armigerous* sons. See *cadency* and *differencing* in the Index.

CADUCEUS (ku-DOO-see-us): The Rod of Hermes or Mercury, around which two *serpents* are entwined. There are two wings near the top and a ball on the upper end. The Caduceus is a symbol of swiftness. It should not be confused with the Rod of *Aesculapius,* but it often is.

CALTRAP, CHEVAL-TRAP, GALTRAP: A device consisting of four

spikes joined together so that, when placed on the ground, one spike is always pointed upward. In battle, caltraps were strewn to penetrate the hooves of *horses*.

CAMEL: The traditional ship of the desert. No doubt for simplicity, the dromedary (one-humped) variety is more usual in heraldry, but the Bactrian (two-humped) has also been used. If you care, you should specify in the *blazon*.

CAMELOPARD (kuh-MELL-oh-PARD): The heraldic word for the giraffe, based on the early belief that this beast was a combination of the *camel* and the *leopard*.

CANNON: Unless the *blazon* specifies otherwise, the old-fashioned muzzle-loader is shown.

CANTING ARMS: A coat of *arms* that contains some reference, often in the form of a pun, to the name of the person bearing them. See Index.

CANTON: A square section of the *shield*, smaller than a *quarter*, in which *augmentations* are often carried. Unless otherwise *blazoned*, a canton appears in the *dexter chief*.

CAP, CHAPEAU (shap-OH): This term refers to a "cap of estate" (see Index). Presumably, one could specify a uniform cap, such as a baseball cap; at best, this is questionable heraldry.

CAP-À-PIE (CAP-ah-PEE): French for "head-to-foot"; used to describe the figure of a man completely encased in armor.

CAPARISONED: Used to describe a *horse* in armor and with a saddle and bridle.

CARPENTER'S SQUARE: The right-angle tool used by carpenters and other craftsmen, an entirely proper and traditional heraldic *charge*. It is usually simply *blazoned* as "a square."

CASTLE: Two towers joined by a wall in the center of which is an arched opening. The towers and the wall are *embattled* (see Figure 32). If there is a third tower over the opening, the *blazon* should call for "a castle triple-towered"; other variations should be *blazoned* accordingly.

CASTOR: Middle English for *beaver*, a useful piece of information for creating *canting* arms. Spelled with a capital C, Castor is a double star in the constellation Gemini. The castor oil plant is, obviously, the source of that substance with so many unpleasant childhood associations. (For that reason, as well as for graphic simplicity, it is probably better to use the beaver than the plant.)

CAT: When the *blazon* specifies a cat, the common household variety is used unless some specific species is named.

CAT-A-MOUNTAIN: The wildcat.

CATHERINE (or Katherine) WHEEL: The instrument on which St. Catherine of Alexandria was martyred. It usually has eight spokes, each ending in a curved spike.

CELESTIAL CROWN: An eight-pointed crown (of which five are visible). Atop each point is a star.

CELESTIAL SPHERE: See *armillary sphere.*

CENTAUR (SEN-tore): The Greek mythological creature with the head, arms, and torso of a man, and the body and legs of a *horse.* When depicted with a *bow* and *arrow,* it is blazoned *Sagittarius* or Sagittary, and is an excellent *charge* as a Zodiac sign.

CHAIN: Usually shown with round or oval links unless otherwise specified in the *blazon.*

CHAPE: See *crampet.*

CHAPEAU: See *cap.*

CHAPLET: A closed circle of leaves with a heraldic *rose* at the top, bottom, and at either side (unless another flower is specified in the *blazon*) ; also called a "garland."

CHARGE: Any design appearing on the *shield* or on another charge. See Index.

CHECKY, CHEQUY, CHECQUY: Describing a *charge* or a *field* divided into small, checkerboard-like squares of alternating *tinctures.* See Figure 17.

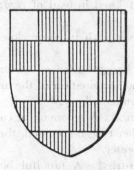

FIG. 17. Checky

CHERUB: The head of a child, with a wing on either side. Use it if you must. The plural is "cherubim."

CHESSROOK: In heraldry, this looks like the chess piece from about the middle down. Its top, however, is bifurcated; that is, divided into two curved points. If you want the *charge* to look like the actual chessrook, the *blazon* should call for a *tower*.

CHESTER HERALD: One of the six *heralds* of the British College of Arms.

CHEVAL-TRAP (sh'VAL) : See *caltrap*.

CHEVALIER (sh'val-YAY) : A rider on a *horse*.

CHEVRON (SHEV-run) : One of the *ordinaries* in the shape of an upside-down letter V. See Figure 4.

CHEVRONEL (shev'ro-NEL) : A narrow *chevron*.

CHEVRONNY (shev-RONNY) : Describing a *field* with an even number of *chevronwise* divisions.

CHEVRONWISE: In the direction of a *chevron*.

CHIEF: An *ordinary* that covers the approximate top third of the *shield*.

CINQUEFOIL (SINK-foil, SANK-foil) : A flowerlike *charge* with five petals.

CLARENCEUX KING OF ARMS: An English heraldic official whose jurisdiction extends south of the River Trent.

CLARION: A now-obscure musical instrument. It is represented as a C-shaped object with a flat top from which five pipes emerge. It is usually *blazoned* "clarion," but is also known as a claricord, clarendon, sufflue, rest, or organ rest, suggesting that as a *charge,* it is probably more trouble than it is worth.

CLIMANT (CLY-mint) : Used instead of *rampant* when describing a *goat*.

CLOSE: Said of a *helmet* with its visor closed, or of a bird with folded wings.

CLOUDS: One of the *charges* whose effectiveness depends to some extent on the skill and imagination of the artist. Invariably, however, clouds are shown as billowy.

COAT ARMOR (or ARMOUR) : A synonym for coat of *arms*.

COCK: Unless some other type is specified, this always refers to the ordinary barnyard rooster.

COCKATRICE (COCK-a-triss) : A fanciful beast that resembles a *wyvern* except that it has a *barbed* tongue emanating from the head of a rooster. See *basilisk*.

COLLAR: If the *blazon* calls for a collar with no further distinction, the depiction is that of a simple band (which may be *charged* and from which various devices may be hung). Special collars depicting knightly orders or badges of office must be specified in the blazon.

COLLARED: Having a *collar* around the neck. Many heraldic animals are shown collared.

COLLEGE OF ARMS: See Index.

COLOMB: The *dove.*

COLORS, COLOURS: The heraldic colors are *Gules, Azure, Sable, Vert,* and *Purpure.* Also see *tinctures, metals, furs,* and Index.

COLUMN: An architectural column; the type should always be specified in the *blazon.* It is sometimes called a "pillar."

COMB: A rooster's crest. Sometimes, however, it refers to a hair comb; the one to be used is discernible from the context.

COMBATANT, COMBATTANT (cum-BAT-tint): Used to describe two *rampant* beasts facing each other; see *respectant.*

COMET: A *star* with light-trails.

COMPARTMENT: The base on which *supporters* stand. See Index.

COMPASSES: In a heraldic *blazon,* this always refers to the mathematical dividers, of which geometry teachers are so fond, used for drawing arcs and circles. They are always shown open and with points at either end.

COMPLEMENT: The full *moon* is described as "the moon in her complement." Sometimes the word "plenitude" is substituted.

COMPONY, COMPONÉ (com-POE-nee): A *charge* consisting of a row of squares of two alternating *tinctures.* For two such rows the proper *blazon* is "counter-compony." For more than two rows, the term is *checky.* This term is variously spelled "gobony," "goboné," and "gobonated."

CONEY: The rabbit. (The popular New York "island" was once believed to have been inhabited by great numbers of coneys.)

CONFRONTÉ: Face to face.

CONJOINED, COJOINED: Touching one another or joined together.

CONTOURNÉ (con-toor-NAY), TOURNÉ: Used to describe a *charge* that has been turned around so that it faces the *sinister.*

CORBIE: The crow or raven. Apart from other possible symbolic uses, it has considerable potential for *canting* arms, as demonstrated in the arms of Corbet of Shropshire.

CORMORANT: The water bird. The *blazon* for the *arms* of the City of Liverpool, quite understandably, describes the cormorant as a "liverbird."

CORNUCOPIA: The horn of plenty; this is the only correct word to use in a *blazon*.

CORONET: See Index.

COTISED: A *bend* with narrow *bendlets* on either side is described as cotised. Other *ordinaries* may also be cotised. The narrow bands are called cotises and, less frequently, cottises, cottices, cottizes, or costs.

COUCHANT (koo-SHAHNT): Said of an animal that is lying down but holding its head erect. See *dormant*.

COUNTER-: A prefix denoting reversal. "Counterchanged," for example, describes a *shield* that is divided by a *line of partition* with the *tinctures* on one side being reversed on the other. (See Figure 18.) Thus, a shield divided down the middle with a *lion rampant* on both sides could have a gold lion on a red background in one half and a red lion on a gold background on the other; in such a shield, the *tinctures* would be counterchanged. Two animals described as "counterpassant" would be shown as *passant* in opposite directions.

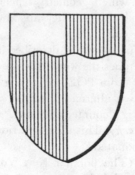

FIG. 18.
Counterchanged

COUPED (coop'd): Cut off. An *ordinary* that is cut off before it reaches the edges of a *shield* is couped; so is a head that is cut off cleanly at the neck.

COURANT, CURRENT: Said of an animal shown running for all it is worth.

COWED, COWARD: Describing an animal with its tail between its legs. This should be regarded as an aesthetic nicety rather than a moral judgment.

CRAMPET: The metal tip at the end of a scabbard that keeps a sword or dagger from poking through. (Also called "boterol" and "chape.")

CRANE: The bird. (See *Heron.*) A good *charge* for *canting* arms.

CRENELLATED, CRENELLÉ: See *embattled.*

CRESCENT: Unless otherwise specified, the points of the crescent always point upward. If they are to point downward, they are *blazoned* "a crescent reversed"; if to the *dexter,* it is *blazoned* "increscent"; if to the *sinister,* "decrescent." In English heraldry the crescent is the mark of *cadency* for the second son.

CREST: A device on top of a *helmet.* See Index.

CRESTED: Having the *comb* of a rooster. Also, one of the *lines of partition,* with little points, like the crests of waves.

CRINED: Referring to the body hair of a person or animal. It is easier to say "crined *sable*" in the *blazon* than to name each of the hairy portions to be colored black.

CROSIER, CROZIER: The staff of office of an abbot or a bishop.

CROSS: See Index and Figure 11.

CROSSBOW: The medieval instrument that shot arrows under power.

CROWN: See Index.

CUBIT ARM: An arm cut off below the elbow.

CUFF: Mentioned in the *blazon* only if its *tincture* differs from that of the sleeve.

CUSHION: A square pillow with a tassle at each corner. If it is to be of any other shape, it must be so *blazoned.*

CYPHER: A monogram. See Index.

DAGGER: In heraldry the dagger looks very much like a sword, except that it is properly depicted with a short and sharply pointed blade.

DAMASKED: A synonym for *diapered.*

DANCETTY, (dan-SETTY) DANCETTÉ, DANCY: One of the *lines of partition.* See Figure 6.

DAVID, SHIELD OF: Usually this Jewish symbol is *blazoned* as "triangles interlaced" but can now probably simply be recorded as the Shield or Star of David. Perhaps the latter term is better in heraldry, to avoid confusion with the heraldic *shield.*

DEBRUISED: When a *charged* field has an *ordinary* or *subordinary* over it, it is said to be debruised.

DECRESCENT: See *crescent*.

DEER: For some reason, a separate vocabulary has evolved for the heraldic deer. Both the specific type of deer and its sex are *blazoned*. A deer's antlers are called *attires;* its points, *tines.* Other animals may be *courant,* but a deer is "in full chase," "at speed," or "in full course." Instead of *passant,* the deer is "trippant"; when *salient,* it is "springing," when *statant guardant,* it is "at gaze."

DEGREES: Steps. An object or structure that is degreed (or sometimes "degraded") is stepped. The number of degrees should be specified in the *blazon.* Often, the term "griece" (variously spelled "greece," "grece") is used.

DELF, DELPH, DELVE: A square *billet.*

DEMI-: A prefix that, when used in conjunction with a *charge,* means only one half of that charge is shown. Unless otherwise specified, it is understood to be the front or upper half.

DEXTER: The left-hand side of a *shield* as you look at it; the right-hand side as seen by the person carrying the shield. Any *charge* that can be placed facing several directions is always shown facing the dexter side unless otherwise specified. See Index.

DIAPER: A pattern or design that covers otherwise plain areas of the *shield* or *charges.* It requires some skill to employ diapering in a coat of *arms* without creating problems of prominence or distinction for the charges. Sometimes called a "damask."

DIFFERENCE, DIFFERENCING: Describing various methods of altering a coat of *arms* so as to distinguish it from other similar arms. See Index.

DISARMED: Used to describe a beast that is to be shown without its armament, such as teeth, claws, horns, etc.

DISMEMBERED: With the limbs severed, but nevertheless in the approximate proper location, with a bit of the *field* showing between the cuts. Why anyone would want such a *charge* is beyond me. It is included here in the interest of scholarship. (Also sometimes blazoned "demembered," or "dechaussé.")

DISPLAYED: Used to describe a bird with its wings spread.

DISTILLING: Shedding drops. In *An Heraldic Alphabet,* J. P.

Brooke-Little refers to a severed head distilling drops of blood and a woman's breast distilling drops of milk. I have never seen the latter *charge* but am willing to bow to his superior knowledge.

Dogs: These are usually *hounds,* but any breed easily depicted will do. See *alan.*

Dolphins: In heraldry, the dolphin in always *embowed* and usually displayed with a tongue emerging from a rather evident beak. Unless otherwise *blazoned,* it is generally shown *naiant.*

Dormant: Asleep; said of animals that are *couchant* but with their heads down and their eyes shut.

Double: A very common prefix meaning two of anything, as in, for example, double-*queued,* having two tails.

Doubled: Used to describing the lining of a *mantling* or a robe.

Dove: The bird.

Dovetail: Describing one of the *lines of partition.* See Figure 6.

Dragon: See Index.

Drops: See *gouttes.*

Eagle: If the *lion* is the king of heraldic beasts, the eagle is surely the king of heraldic birds. See Index.

Ecclesiastical Hat: See Index.

Eightfoil: The *octofoil.*

Embattled: Describing one of the *lines of partition* consisting of alternating squares with open upper and lower ends. (See Figure 6.) Sometimes the terms "crenellated," "crenellé," "battled," and "imbattled" are used.

Emblazon: To paint a coat of *arms* with its proper colors. *Blazoning* is describing; "emblazoning" is painting.

Embowed: Curved or bent in an archlike position; usually used to describe fish or human arms.

Embrued, Imbrued: Bloody; frequently used to describe weapons.

Encircled: Used to describe a *serpent* coiled in a circle (also "involved" and "voluted"). "Encircled by," however, means exactly what it does in ordinary English.

Endorsed: See *addorsed.*

Enflamed, Inflamed: Flaming (also, "fired" or "flamant").

Engrailed: A *line of partition* with downward scallops. See Figure 6.

Enhanced: Said of an *ordinary* that is placed higher than its normal position. (Also "hausé," "haussé.")

ENSIGNED: Said of a *charge* that has some insigne, such as a *crown*, placed over it.

ENTIRE: Used to describe a *charge* that reaches the edges of a *shield* when it would not ordinarily do so. (Also, "throughout.")

ENVIRONED: A synonym for *encircled*.

EQUIPPED: See *cap-à-pie* and *caparisoned*.

ERADICATED: A devastatingly accurate term to describe a *tree* which has been torn out by its roots and which, typically, has the roots showing.

ERASED: Technically, this term refers to the jagged ends of the neck of a beast or person whose head has been indelicately removed from the rest of the body. In practice, however, an erased head has almost feathery edges where the actual decapitation is supposed to have taken place and makes for a rather attractive *charge*.

ERECT: In a vertical or upright position; especially applicable to a *charge* that would not normally be so placed.

ERMINE, ERMINES, ERMINOIS (ermin-WAH): Heraldic *furs*. See Index.

ESCALLOP: The sea scallop shell. It is the symbol of St. James of Compostella and is also associated with pilgrims, who frequently used them as a kind of all-purpose utensil. It is an attractive *charge*. A *field* that has escallops scattered all over it is said to be "escallopé."

ESCUTCHEON: A synonym for *shield*. See Figure 19.

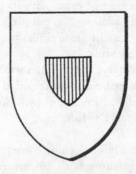

FIG. 19.
Escutcheon

ESQUIRE: The right-hand man and *shield*-bearer of a knight. In general, the esquire's *helmet* is used by individuals assuming coats of *arms* who cannot prove the descent from nobles or titled individuals that entitles them to another kind of helmet. See Index.

ESTOIL (ES-toyl, es-TWAHL): A star with wavy lines resembling a starfish. Unless otherwise *blazoned,* it is drawn with six points. A *field* scattered with stars is described as "estoilé." See *mullet.*

FACED: *Caboshed lions* and *leopards* are correctly *blazoned* as faced; however, if you use *caboshed,* no one will complain.

FALCHION: A sword with a broad blade; the cutting edge is curved, the back is straight. It is related to the *scimitar* and *seax.*

FALCON: The bird; actually, several birds. Often, despite the specificity of a *blazon,* falcons and *hawks* come out looking alike. They are often shown *jessed* and *belled.*

FAN: This term applies equally to the fan frequently associated with delicate ladies given to fits of the vapors and to the winnowing fan more familiar to agricultural types. The *blazon* should specify which kind.

FASCES (FASS-eez): A bundle of rods tied together around an ax with its blade projecting. In ancient Rome, it was borne by magistrates as a symbol of authority, and is a good *charge* for individuals involved with the judiciary. (It can be seen on the reverse side of Liberty-head dimes.)

FEATHER: Widely used throughout heraldry. *Peacock* and *ostrich* feathers are most common. In any case, the type of feather should be given in the *blazon.*

FEATHERED: Describing the feathers of an *arrow.* Also, "flighted."

FER-DE-MOLINE, FER-DE-MOULINE: See *mill rind.*

FERRATED: Strewn with *horseshoes.* Authorities claim that this is a rarely used *charge,* but it has distinct possibilities. It derives from "ferr," a little used synonym for horseshoe.

FESS, FESSE: One of the *ordinaries;* a wide horizontal stripe across the middle of the *shield* and, as with most other ordinaries, occupying approximately one third of the space. See Figure 4.

FESS POINT: The *shield's* center.

FESSWISE: In the direction of the *fess.*

FETTERLOCK, FETLOCK: A device used for hobbling *horses,* consisting of an iron cylinder and a U-shaped piece that is hinged on one end of the cylinder and locked on the other. It is usually shown closed unless *blazoned* otherwise.

FIELD: The surface of the *shield*. See Index.

FIMBRIATED: Having a narrow edge or border, the *tincture* of which differs from that of the rest of the *charge*.

FINNED: Used when a *fish's* fins are of a *lincture* that differs from that of the rest of its body.

FIRE BALL: A sphere with flames coming out of four sides in a crosslike pattern.

FIRED: See *enflamed*.

FISH: Chances are that if it is found in the water, it can be found in heraldry. See Index.

FITCHY, FITCHÉ, FITCHED: Tapering to a point at the foot; usually, but not necessarily, applicable to *crosses*.

FLAMANT: See *enflamed*.

FLAMBEAU: Synonym for *torch*.

FLANCHES, FLAUNCHES, FLANQUES, FLASQUES: Two curved lines coming from the upper corners of the *shield* and ending at the *dexter* and *sinister* sides. They are always in pairs.

FLEAM, FLEME, FLEGME: An ancient razorlike instrument with a curved handle. It looks rather like a stylized "7" and seems to be popular among those who practice medicine.

FLECTED, FLEXED: Bent; used to describe an arm or leg.

FLEECE: The term apparently is intended to describe the hide of a horned *ram*. It is always shown with a band around its middle, to which is affixed a ring. It hangs as though it were suspended from a hook and is a fitting *charge* for butchers, and, possibly, those in various aspects of the wool industry. See *Agnus Dei*.

FLESHPOT: A round, three-legged cauldron. An attractive *charge* with a number of applications, although possibly causing some embarrassment through misinterpretation of its symbolism.

FLEUR-DE-LIS, FLEUR-DE-LYS: The stylized lily so often associated with France. See Index.

FLEURY, FLORY: Describing a *charge* that is either decorated with *fleurs-de-lis* or ends in a fleur-de-lis.

FLIGHTED: See *feathered*.

FLOTANT: Floating; describes either a ship or a flag.

FLOWERS: Considerable flora flourish in heraldry. See Index.

FLUKE: The pointed or *barbed* tip of an *anchor*.

FOLIATED: Having leaves.

FORCENE, FORCENÉ (for-SEEN, FOR-sin-NAY): Describing a rearing *horse;* often, and always incorrectly, used to describe a horse *rampant.*

FORMY, FORMÉ: A type of cross. See Figure 11.

FOUNTAIN: A fountain is always a *roundel barry wavy Argent Azure;* in other words, in a circle, wavy stripes of alternating white and blue. If a so-called "natural" fountain is desired, it could be carefully indicated in the *blazon.*

FOURCHÉ (foor-SHAY): Forked, as when describing a forked tail.

FOX: The animal. See Index.

FOX'S MASK: The face of a *fox* that has been *caboshed.*

FRACTED: Broken.

FRAISE, FRASE, FRAZE: The *cinquefoil* so *blazoned* when it is intended to mean the flower of the strawberry in *canting* arms.

FRET: A *mascle* interlaced with *bendlets dexter* and *sinister;* in other words, a diamond shape with diagonal lines running through it. See Figure 20.

FIG. 20. Fret

FRETTY: Interlaced *bendlets* running *dexter* and *sinister* to form a diamond-shaped pattern somewhat resembling a trellis. See Figure 21.

FIG. 21. Fretty

FRUCTED: Fruit-bearing. A *tree* is often described as "fructed" if its fruit or nuts are depicted.

FUMANT (FYOO-mint): Sending out smoke.

FURS: *Ermine* and *Vair* are the principal furs. See Index.

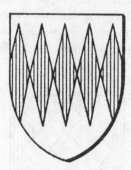

FIG. 22. Fusils

FUSIL: An elongated diamond shape. See Figure 22; see *lozenge*.

FUSILLY: A pattern of near-horizontal diamond shapes resulting from crossing diagonals. The sections are somewhat narrower than those referred to by "lozengy"; see *lozenge*.

GALLEY: See *lymphad*.

GALTRAP: See *caltrap*.

GARB: A sheaf of grain, always shown tied with a band. (Unless another grain is specified, a garb usually refers to a sheaf of wheat.)

GARDANT: See *guardant*.

GARLAND: See *chaplet*.

GARTER: A circular strap with a buckle at the bottom *pendant*, or hanging down.

GARTER KING OF ARMS: The principal English heraldic officer.

GATE: Generally depicted as having three to five horizontal bars, a diagonal crosspiece, and hinges. It is not an especially attractive *charge*, but may be desirable in *canting* arms or those associated with a profession or occupation.

GAUNTLET: As styles of armor varied, so did the style of gauntlet, the protective glove worn by knights in combat. It is therefore shown in various ways in heraldry. The *blazon* should indicate whether it is the *sinister* or *dexter* gauntlet.

GEM RING: A ring with a single stone in it.

GEMEL (JEM'l) RING, GIMMEL RING, GIMBAL RING: Two or more rings interlaced to form one whole ring.

GIRAFFE: In heraldry, the giraffe is called a *camelopard*.

GLISSANT: Describing the movements of *serpents*.

GLOBE: Generally, this refers to the earth. There are, however, opportunities for misinterpretations; it is better, therefore, to *blazon* a *terrestrial globe*.

GOAT: Unless otherwise *blazoned*, the common billy goat, complete with horns and beard, is shown. See *climant*.

GOBONY: See *compony*.

GORGED: A synonym for *collared*.

GOUTTE (goot): A drop, as of water, blood, milk, etc.

GOUTTY, GOUTTÉ, GUTTY, GUTTÉ: Scattered with drops. Unfortunately, heraldists apparently allowed their romantic tendencies to get the better of them when *blazoning* goutty fields or charges. Thus, instead of *goutty gules* for "scattered with red drops," they prefer phrases like *goutty de sang*, "scattered with drops of blood." If you come across such phrases in a blazon, do the best you can. For your own blazon, stick with "goutty," followed by the *tincture*.

GRANT OF ARMS: The bestowal of a coat of *arms* by a proper authority. See Index.

GRAPPLING IRON: A device used to hold two ships together. It closely resembles an *anchor* except that it has four prongs.

GREECES, GRECES, GRIECES: See *degrees*.

GRENADE: A ball with flames coming from the top. (Also called a "bomb.")

GREYHOUND: The greyhound is depicted as it exists in real life and assumes the various poses common to heraldic beasts. See *dogs*.

GRIFFIN, GRYPHON: A mythical monster that frequently appears in heraldry. See Index.

GUARDANT, GARDANT (GAR-dunt): Used to describe a creature facing outward toward the observer. The position of the body is always given first, and then that of the head. Thus, a lion *passant guardant* has three paws on the ground, one paw upraised, and its face turned toward you.

FIG. 23.

Rampant guardant

GULES (gyoolz): Red. Abbreviated g. or gu. See Index.

GUNSTONE, GUNSHOT: A black *roundel;* also, "pellet."

GURGES (GURJ'z): A whirlpool, shown as concentric rings starting at the center of the *field* and extending to the outer edges. Also *blazoned* "gorge."

GYRON (JY-run): When a *quarter* is divided diagonally by a line from the *dexter chief* (upper left) to the *fess point* (center of the shield), the lower half of that quarter is called a gyron. It is wedge-shaped, with a straight horizontal line along the bottom and a diagonal line along the side. See Figure 5.

GYRONNY (ji-RONNY): Dividing the *shield* into four equally placed *gyrons,* resulting in eight sections. (If there are to be fewer or more sections, the *blazon* must so state: "gyronny of ten," etc.)

HABITED: Clothed; sometimes *blazoned* "vested."

HAFTED: Having a handle like those found on axes or spears.

HALBERD: A weapon that combines an ax and a spear on a long shaft. It has proven useful in *canting arms,* as Halbert's of heraldry-merchandising fame proved.

HAMMER: Typically, one with a wooden handle and a metal head and ball, unless some specific variety is *blazoned.*

HAND: Unless otherwise *blazoned,* the right hand is always shown, *apaumé* and *couped* at the wrist. To be on the safe side, the *blazon* should give a detailed description. See *benediction.*

HARP: An excellent *charge* for people of Irish descent, the harp may be shown in virtually any manner. It is a good idea, therefore, to give some detail in the *blazon.*

HARPY: In mythology, a monster with the head and breasts of a woman on the body of a vulture. It appears as a heraldic *charge;* no doubt those who used it had their reasons.

HART: A variety of *deer,* ideally suited for *canting* arms.

HATCHING: The system of lines and dots that represents the *tinctures* in heraldry, such as in black-and-white printing and in engraved metals. See Index and Figure 10.

HATCHMENT: The heraldic *achievement* painted on a large *lozenge* and placed outside the home of one who has died, during the mourning period. Many hatchments were then hung in churches where they may be seen today throughout England.

HAURIENT (rhymes with "Orient"): Said of a *fish* placed vertically with its head up.

HAWK: The bird; a good *charge* for *canting* arms. See *falcon.*

HAWK'S BELL: A round bell with a ball inside it.

HEAD: There are various customs for depicting the human head. An Englishman's head, for example, is usually shown with blond hair, moustache, and beard. If the *blazon* does not specify the precise positioning, the head is usually drawn in profile, facing right and *couped.* If you insist on including a human head in your coat of *arms,* it is best to be very explicit in the blazon.

HEART: Another good *charge* for *canting* arms, in addition to its other obvious symbolism. It is always depicted as the familiar playing-card type of heart.

HEATER SHIELD: The most commonly used *shield* pattern; so called because it somewhat resembles the sole of a flatiron. See Chapter 14 and Index.

HEDGEHOG: The animal. It is also known as a *herisson,* "heri-zon," "urchin," and "urcheon."

HELMET, HELM, HEAUME: The helmet is a traditional component of a heraldic *achievement.* Some believe that it is necessary if a *crest* is to be included. In British and other heraldic systems there are elaborate rules as to which style of helmet should be used and how it should be placed, depending upon one's rank. See Index.

HELVE: See *hafted.*

HERALD: A heraldic officer. See Index.

HERALDS' COLLEGE: A synonym for College of Arms. See Index.

HERISSON, HERIZON: French for *hedgehog;* persons named Harris, Harrison, or variations of those names could use the hedgehog as a *charge* and, for *canting* purposes, *blazon* it "herrison."

HERMES, ROD OF: See *Caduceus.*

HERON: The bird. There appears to be some confusion among heraldic artists over herons, *cranes,* and storks. Strictly speaking, the heron (unlike the stork) has a crest of long feathers toward the back of its head, while the crane sports longer tail feathers and a longer neck than either the stork or the heron. The heron (like the crane and the stork) is *blazoned* "in its vigilance" when it stands on one leg and holds a stone in the upraised claw.

HERRING: The fish, usually drawn as in life. There appear to be no records for *blazoning* one that has been pickled.

HILT: The handle of a *sword, dagger,* etc., which generally includes the guard as well. The knob at the end of the hilt is called a "pommel." If the hilt and/or pommel are of a *tincture* that is different from the rest of the sword, these are described as "hilted" or "pommelled," and followed by the specific tincture.

HIND: The animal. See *deer.*

HIPPOCAMPUS: If you plan to use a sea horse in your coat of *arms* and want it to appear as it does in nature, the *blazon* should read "a sea horse (hippocampus)"; otherwise, you are likely to end up with a grotesque creature that has the upper half of a *horse* and the lower half of a *fish.*

HIPPOGRIFF: A creature whose upper half is that of a female *griffin* and whose nether parts are those of a *horse.*

HOLY LAMB: See *Agnus Dei.*

HONOR POINT: A point located between the top of the *shield* and the *fess point;* i.e., in the center of the approximate upper third of the shield. See Figure 2.

HONORARY ARMS: *Arms* granted by the English heraldic authorities to persons who are not British citizens but who can prove direct descent in the male line from a British subject. See Index.

HOOFED: Used when describing the hoofs of an animal when they are of another *tincture.* Synonyms are "unguled" and "onglé."

HORN: See *bugle horn.*

HORN OF PLENTY: See *cornucopia.*

HORNED: Used to describe the horns of animals, although *armed* is the more frequently seen synonym.

HORNS: The horns of animals; also, the points of a *crescent.*

HORSE: When a horse is to be shown rearing, it is *blazoned* as *forcene;* otherwise its positions are described in the same terms as used for other animals. For reasons now obscure, the head of a horse is usually *blazoned* "a nag's head." Should you choose to ignore this nicety, few will call you to task for it.

HORSESHOE: The heraldic horseshoe is of the ordinary variety and, superstition notwithstanding, is shown with the open end downward (unless specifically *blazoned* otherwise). Sometimes a horseshoe is blazoned "ferr." See *ferrated.*

HOUNDS: The *greyhound* and the *talbot* (good for *canting* arms) appear frequently in heraldry.

HUITFOIL (WHEAT-foil): An eight-petaled flower. See *octofoil.*

HUMETTY, HUMMETTÉ (hew-MET-tee): *Couped* at the ends. The cut ends usually adhere to the adjacent contours of the *shield.* A *bar* humetty is called a "humet" or a "hamade."

HUNTING HORN: See *bugle horn.*

HURST: A group of *trees.*

HURT, HEURT: A blue *roundel.*

HURTY, HURTÉ: Scattered with *hurts.*

HYDRA: A seven-headed *dragon.*

IBEX: The heraldic *antelope,* but with straight, serrated horns that point forward.

IMBATTLED: See *embattled.*

IMBRUED: See *embrued.*

IMPALE: To take the halves of two coats of *arms* and combine them into a new, single coat of arms. See Index.

IMPERIAL EAGLE: Because it was the emblem of the Holy Roman

Empire, the double-headed *eagle* is sometimes called the Imperial Eagle. See Index.

INCENSED: Shooting fire, especially with regard to *dragons, panthers,* etc., with flames coming from their mouths and ears.

INDIVISIBLE ARMS: *Arms* which, by virtue of design or grant, cannot be divided; also called "impartible arms."

INDORSED: See *addorsed.*

IN ESCUTCHEON: A *shield* that is placed as a *charge* on another shield is called "in escutcheon." See Index.

INFLAMED: See *enflamed.*

IN FOLIAGE: Having leaves, as a *tree* or plant.

INGRAILED: See *engrailed.*

IN PRETENCE: When *arms* are borne *in escutcheon* on other arms, they are said to be in pretence.

IN PRIDE: Describing the outspread tail of a *peacock.*

IN SPLENDOR: Used to describe the sun and its rays. Sometimes shown as "in glory." See *sun.*

INTERCHANGED: Synonym for *counterchanged.*

INVECTED: A scalloped *line of partition* with the rounded portions facing upward. See Figure 6.

INVERTED: Turned upside down.

INVOLVED: See *encircled; serpent.*

IRRADIATED: Surrounded by light rays.

ISSUANT: Issuing out of.

JAMB, GAMB: A beast's leg.

JAVELIN: In heraldry, the javelin is short and *barbed.*

JELLOPED: When a rooster's wattles are *tinctured* differently from the body, they are described as "wattled" or "jelloped." For example, a *blazon* could call for *"a cock Argent, beaked, legged, combed, and jelloped Gules,"* resulting in a white rooster with the named appurtenances in red.

JESSANT-DE-LIS (je-SANN-duh-LEE): With a *fleur-de-lis* shooting out. A well-known *charge* is "a *leopard's* face, *jessant-de-lis";* it shows the head of a leopard behind which is seen a fleur-de-lis whose base emanates from the creature's mouth. This is another charge that would seem to beg for a good reason for modern usage.

JESSED: Said of a *hawk, falcon,* or other hunting bird that has a short strap around its leg to which a leash might be attached.

KEY: A popular *charge* that comes in so many variations that the specific type and its precise position should be indicated in the *blazon*. See Index.

KING OF ARMS: A principal heraldic authority.

KNOT: Traditionally, knots are used as *badges* rather than *charges* and some have come to be associated with specific families. Nevertheless, almost any readily identifiable mariner's knot could serve as a charge as long as it *is* readily identifiable—not too complicated and, of course, specified in the *blazon*.

LABEL: A horizontal band with three vertical pieces hanging from it. (If more or fewer points are desired, the *blazon* must so indicate.) A label has been used as a *mark of difference*. See Index and Figure 8.

LAMB: An excellent *charge* for *canting arms* or arms representing an occupation. See also *Agnus Dei* and *fleece*.

LAMINATED: Scaled, as a *fish* or *serpent*.

LANCASTER HERALD: An English heraldic officer.

LANGUED (lang'd) : Tongued; that is, when the tongue of a creature is of a *tincture* that is different from the rest of the body. See *lion*.

LATIN CROSS: A *cross* with a shaft that is considerably longer than the other limbs; also called "long cross" and "passion cross."

LEAF: Virtually any kind of identifiable leaf is a suitable *charge* as long as the type is named in the *blazon*. See *slipped*.

LEG: The human leg is usually shown bent at the knee.

LEGGED: A synonym for *membered*.

LEOPARD: Originally, a *lion passant guardant* was blazoned as a leopard. These days, however, the word properly describes the real thing.

LEOPARD'S FACE: See *caboshed*.

LILY: The flower; not to be confused with the *fleur-de-lis*. The "natural" lily is nevertheless depicted with stylized simplicity rather than botanical accuracy.

LINED: Referring to a leash or a line on a *charge*. A beast may be "*collared* and lined." When referring to the *mantling*, this term is sometimes used, but *doubled* is more common.

LINES OF PARTITION: The lines that divide the *shield* or any of the *charges* into sections. Each line of partition is preceded by *per* and the *ordinary* in whose direction the line goes. Thus, *per fess wavy* indicates a horizontal wavy line across the middle of the shield. See Figure 6.

LION: The unchallenged king of the heraldic beasts. Its popularity and frequency of appearance are measures of its sovereignty. The claws and tongue of a lion are usually red (*armed* and *langued gules*) unless the beast is red or placed on a red background, in which case he is usually *armed* and *langued azure*. Any variations, therefore, must be *blazoned* accordingly. See Index.

LION'S FACE: See *caboshed*.

LIVER BIRD: See *cormorant*.

LIVERY: If you are rich enough to have servants who wear uniforms, you may want to dress them in the principal *color* and *metal* of your coat of arms. If that strikes you as a trifle pretentious, you can use these *tinctures* for your racing silks.

LIZARD: A perfectly acceptable heraldic *charge*. See *lynx*.

LONGBOW: The well-known medieval arrow-shooter; a good *charge* for people named Archer.

LONG CROSS: See *Latin Cross*.

LOTUS: Heraldically, the flower is almost always stylized. Its depiction is usually left up to the artist.

LOZENGE (LOZZ-inj) : Any diamond shape; typically, it is a square standing on one corner. Long and narrow diamonds are called *fusils*. A *shield* or area divided into a pattern of lozenges is termed "lozengy" (accent on second syllable).

LUCE, LUCY: This *fish* is now known as a *pike* except in heraldic *blazons*.

LYMPHAD: The heraldic word for *galley*. It should always be *blazoned* "with sails furled" or "in full sail." If it is adorned with flags and *pennons*, this, too, should be specified. "Oars in action" indicates that the lymphad is being rowed.

LYNX: A member of the cat family that is a perfectly acceptable heraldic *charge* (it is now used by an English family named Lynch), but, in ancient *blazons*, it was synonymous with "lizard." Be careful.

LYON KING OF ARMS: The chief Scottish heraldic officer.

MACE: This word now has several meanings. As a weapon, it was a club at the head of which was a spiked ball. It is also a ceremonial staff carried as a symbol of authority and the name of a spice. Any of these are acceptable *charges*, but the *blazon* must be very specific. (The chemical used to repel muggers and rioters has no place in heraldry.)

MALLET, MARTEL: Unless the *blazon* specifies the type of mallet, the artist will draw an ordinary wooden hammer.

MANCH: See *maunche*.

MANED: Used in describing an animal's mane. See *crined*.

MAN LION: A creature with a *lion's* body and a human face.

MANTICORE (MAN-tikor): A monster with a man's head, *lion's* body, and the tail of a *scorpion* or *dragon*. There are variations on the theme. In heraldry, the body is typically that of a *tyger*. Sometimes the manticore has two spiral horns. It is also known as a "mantiger." It is a singularly ugly charge.

MANTLE, MANTLING: The stylized cape attached to the *helmet* and flowing around and behind the *shield*. See Chapter 14 and Index.

MAPLE LEAF: Typically, the red maple leaf is associated with Canada.

MARKS OF CADENCY: See *cadency* and Index.

MARKS OF DIFFERENCE: See *difference* and Index.

MARSHALLING: The combining of more than one coat of *arms*. See Index.

FIG. 24. Mascles

MARTEL: See *mallet*.

MARTLET: A peculiarly heraldic bird which looks somewhat like a martin but has no legs. In British heraldry it is the mark of *cadency* for a fourth son.

MASCLE, MACLE: A *voided lozenge;* that is, a diamond shape in outline. In British heraldry, it is the mark of a divorcée. See Figure 24.

MASCULY: Consisting of connected *mascles.*

MASONED: Used to describe a *charge* drawn to look like brickwork. If the separating lines between the bricks have a *tincture* that differs from the charge (as opposed to simply being shaded with a darker color), the *blazon* specifies "masoned of" followed by the tincture of the lines.

MAUNCH, MAUNCHE, MANCH: A sleeve with a long, pendulant cuff. It frequently resembles a "7." See Index.

MELUSINE: A two-tailed *mermaid* with a totally unbelievable story. See Index.

MEMBERED: Used in describing the beaks and legs of birds when they are of a *tincture* that is different from that of the body. "Legged" is a synonym.

MERCURY, ROD OF: See *Caduceus.*

MERMAID: Half woman, half fish; see Index and *Melusine.*

MERMAN: Half man, half fish; see Index and *Neptune, Triton.*

METALS: The heraldic metals are *Or* (gold) and *Argent* (silver). See Index.

MIDAS'S HEAD: The head of a bearded, long-haired man with the ears of an ass. Why anyone would want to use such a *charge* is beyond me.

MILL RIND: The piece of iron placed in the center of a millstone. Its exact shape is left up to the heraldic artist. It is also known as a "mill iron," "fer-de-moline," "fer-de-mouline," and "ink moline."

MITRE: The traditional clerical headgear. Its use in heraldry is usually reserved for those members of the clergy entitled to wear it.

MOLET: See *mullet.*

MONOGRAM: See *cypher.*

MONSTER: Any creature that does not exist in the real world is heraldically classified as a monster.

MOON: The full moon is *blazoned* "in her *complement*" or "in *plenitude.*" To distinguish it from a *plate,* it is often shown with a face. A moon that is not full is a *crescent.* See Index.

MORION (MOR-ee-on): A caplike metal *helmet* with curved peaks front and rear and a *crest* along the top, worn by soldiers in the sixteenth and seventeenth centuries. Although not a frequently used *charge,* it seems suitable to those who can trace their ancestry back to the days of the *conquistadores,* with whom this helmet is associated in American history.

MORT'S HEAD: A skull. *Mort* is French for death. As a *charge,* it is startling, to say the least, and could serve for *canting* arms for someone with a bizarre sense of humor or with a pirate or two in his ancestry (in which case, the more proper *blazon* would probably be "skull and crossbones").

MOTTO: A battle cry or inspirational saying written on a ribbonlike scroll usually (but not always) placed beneath the coat of arms. See Index.

MOUNT: A hill, which, when used as a *charge,* is invariably placed at the bottom of the *shield* and is *blazoned* "a mount in *base."* It is also used as the base for a *crest.* (Be careful not to *blazon* this charge as "a mound," which is a ball with a cross on top. It is the emblem of English sovereignty. If you are entitled to display a mound, you probably have no need for this book.)

MOUNTAIN CAT: This is the term to use in the *blazon* if you want this specific kind of cat to be drawn. See *cat; cat-a-mountain.*

MOUNTED: Used to describe a *horse* that has a rider.

MULLET, MOULET: A five-pointed star. (See *estoil.*) The term derives from the French *moulette* and originally meant the *rowel* of a *spur.* If you want your *charge* to resemble the original more closely, you must indicate in the *blazon* the number of points (six should do it) and that the mullet is *pierced,* so that it will be drawn with a hole in the middle. A mullet is also a type of *fish,* and if that is the charge intended, it must be so stated in the blazon. Probably "mullet fish" would suffice.

MURAL CROWN, MURAL CORONET: A crown that resembles an *embattled* wall. It is an appropriate *charge* for those who are proud of a distinguished military career. See *crown* and Index.

MURREY: One of the so-called *stains* in the heraldic paintbox. It is defined as a mulberry color, a kind of red-purple.

MUZZLED: Used in describing an animal wearing a muzzle.

NAG'S HEAD: A horse's head. See *horse.*

NAIANT (NAY-int), NATANT: Swimming, used in describing *fish* that appear to be swimming across the *field.*

NAIANT COUNTER-NAIANT: Swimming in opposite directions.

NAIL: Usually shown without the head and, for obvious reasons, frequently *blazoned* "passion nail."

NAISSANT (NAY-sint): Describing a creature emerging from the middle of one of the *ordinaries;* not to be confused with *issuant.*

NAVEL POINT: Synonym for *nombril point.*

NEBULY, NEBULÉ (NEB-you-lee): One of the *lines of partition,* a kind of dovetailed effect but with rounded corners. See Index and Figure 6.

NEEDLE: This homely object makes an excellent *charge.*

NEPTUNE: The Roman sea god and the eighth *planet* from the sun. Unless otherwise *blazoned,* Neptune is depicted as a *merman* wearing a *crown* and carrying a *trident.* Also see *triton.*

NERVED: Synonym for "veined"; refers to the veins of a *leaf.*

NIMBUS: A halo; sometimes *blazoned* "glory."

NOMBRIL POINT, NAVEL POINT: A point of the *shield* located in the center—in other words, just about where the shield's navel would be if it were a torso.

NORROY KING OF ARMS: An English heraldic officer.

NOWED: Knotted; usually applied to animals' tails and *serpents'* bodies when tied in a knot.

NOWY: One of the *lines of partition;* a straight line interrupted by arcs. See Figure 6.

OAK: The symbolic solidity of the oak tree makes it a fine *charge.* Oak branches are also frequently used. To include a few acorns, the *blazon* should specify *fructed.*

OCTOFOIL: A flowerlike design similar to the *cinquefoil* but with eight petals, which makes it something of a mystery as to why this should be the mark of *cadency* for the ninth son.

OFFICER OF ARMS: Any of the thirteen Kings, Heralds, and Pursuivants comprising the English College of Arms, or of the seven officers of the Scottish heraldic authority.

OGRESS: A black *roundel;* also called a "pellet."

ONDÉ: Synonym for *undy.*

ONGLÉ: Synonym for *hoofed.*

OPINICUS: A monster with the head, neck, and wings of a *griffin,* the body of a *lion,* and the tail of a *bear.* It appears in the *arms* of two trade guilds, the Barber-Surgeons' Company, and in a somewhat different version, the Plaisterers' Company, both of

London, a fact that may prove useful to barbers, surgeons, and plasterers who want to design their own coats of arms.

OPPRESSED: Synonym for *debruised.*

OR: Gold or yellow. See Index.

ORANGE: The fruit has been used as a *charge* and, of course, can be again. A word of caution: If you are dealing with a heraldic artist steeped in history and tradition, he may render an orange as a *roundel tenné;* that is, an orange-colored disc, which is a correct but rarely used form.

ORB: Synonym for "mound." See *mount.*

ORDINARIES: The term applied to certain basic *charges* consisting primarily of *bars,* bands, and stripes. Sometimes, smaller versions of the ordinaries are called *subordinaries.* Other geometric shapes such as the *lozenge, fusil, billet, roundel,* etc. are also termed subordinaries. Ordinaries occupy about one third of the *shield.* See Figures 4 and 5 and Index.

ORGAN-REST: A synonym for *clarion.*

ORLE: Similar to a *bordure* except that it does not reach the edges of the *shield.* In effect, it is an outline shape following the shape of the shield so that the edges of the shield form a kind of margin around the orle. When *charges* are placed on the shield in the pattern of an orle they are *blazoned* "an orle of" or "in orle." Thus, *"mullets, Argent* in orle" or "an orle of mullets Argent" mean a series of silver stars placed along, but not touching, the edges of the shield. It is a good idea to include in the blazon the number of the charges placed "in orle."

OSTRICH: Although the bird appears as a *charge,* its *feathers,* generally drawn with a curled end, is much more frequent. If the *quill* is *tinctured* differently from the feather, it is *blazoned* "quilled" or "penned." This holds true for other feathers as well.

OTTER: This aquatic mammal, perhaps best known for its good-natured playfulness and, unfortunately, for its fur, makes a suitable *charge.*

OVER ALL: Describing a *charge* that is placed over other charges; often used to *blazon* an *escutcheon.*

OWL: Obviously, a personal favorite. It is usually drawn as shown in the Frontispiece, with its body in profile (the *blazon* indicating whether the *dexter* or *sinister* side shows) and the face frontward, unless otherwise blazoned. If a particular species of owl is required, this must also be specified in the blazon. See Index.

Ox: The heraldic ox looks like a *bull,* but for your own reasons you may prefer the former in the *blazon.*

PADLOCK: This useful and attractive *charge* will be drawn according to the artist's fancy unless a specific type is given in the *blazon.*

PAIRLE: French for *pall;* for some reason, it has lately been showing up in English heraldry.

PALE: One of the *ordinaries.* It is a vertical band occupying the approximate center third of the *shield.* See Figure 4.

PALEWISE: In the direction of the *pale;* that is, vertically down the middle as in "palewise three mullets Argent," three silver stars down the middle of the *shield.*

PALL: A kind of *subordinary* that can best be described as resembling the letter Y. The vertical portion is somewhat longer than the two angular ones. Also *shakefork.*

PALMER'S STAFF: See *bourdon.*

PALY: Divided *palewise* into an even number of sections. "Paly *barry*" would result in a checkerboard effect. "Paly *bendy*" also gives a checkerboard effect, but with elongated diamond shapes.

PANACHE (puh-NASH): A group of *feathers* usually worn as the *crest* on a *helmet.* In heraldry, unless otherwise *blazoned,* it is shown as three rows of *ostrich* feathers. In non-heraldic usage, the word implies a certain verve, a certain amount of dash. Thus, the panache is a good *charge,* especially if it fits the personality.

PANTHER: In heraldry, the panther is a *cat* that is usually *incensed* (i.e., with flames coming from its ears and mouth). It is often spotted. If you have some other beast in mind, such as the black panther or mountain lion, it is best to specify because in everyday usage, "panther" applies to several feline varieties.

PARROT: When *blazoned proper,* the parrot is drawn with a green head and body and red legs and feet. (Strictly speaking, the *blazon* should call for a "popinjay," but no one will criticize you too severely for staying with more familiar nomenclature.)

PARTED: A synonym for *party.*

PARTITION, LINES OF: See *Lines of Partition* and Index.

PARTY, PARTED: Divided. Used to indicate how a *shield* is to be divided. "Parted *fesswise*" or "party per *fess*" means that the shield is divided through the middle by a horizontal line. The phrase is followed by the *tinctures* of each of the parts. A shield may be divided "party per *saltire*," "per *chevron*," etc.

PASCHAL LAMB: See *Agnus Dei*.

PASSANT: Describing an animal walking with its right forepaw raised and bent at the knee. "*Counter*passant" describes two animals walking in opposite directions. See Figure 25 and *trippant*.

FIG. 25.

Passant

PASSION NAIL: See *nail*.

PASTORAL STAFF: See *crosier*.

PATY, PATÉ, PATTÉ: A type of *cross* perhaps best typified by the German Iron Cross. Also *blazoned* "formy" and "formé."

PAVILION: Usually, a synonym for *tent*. See Index.

PAW: The foot of an animal, severed at the first joint; it is, therefore, shorter than the *jamb*.

PAWN: Although I have not come across this chesspiece as a *charge*, I see no reason for its not being used. It is probably best *blazoned* "chess pawn" because "pawne" is a (rarely used) heraldic synonym for *peacock*.

PEACOCK: Unless otherwise *blazoned*, the peacock is drawn facing *dexter* and with its tail closed. "A peacock in his pride" is shown *affronty* with its tail spread.

PEAN: A *fur* with gold spots scattered on a black background; one of the *tinctures*. See Index.

PEA-RISE, PEASE RISE: A pea stalk with flowers and leaves.

PEGASUS (PEG-asus): The familiar winged *horse* of Greek mythology, lately identified as the trademark of a gasoline company.

PELICAN: Unless otherwise *blazoned*, this estimable creature is almost always shown *vulning;* that is, with wings raised and pecking at its breast. The pelican is also blazoned "in her piety," in which case it is shown surrounded by its young who are feeding on its blood. See Index.

PELLET: See *gunstone.*

PELLETY: Strewn with *pellets.*

PENCIL: A synonym for *pennoncelle.*

PENDANT, PENDENT: Drooping or hanging down from.

PENNED: See *ostrich.*

PENNON, PENNANT: A long, triangular flag flown from a lance.

PENNONCELLE, PENCELL, PENCIL, PENSELL, PINSIL: A shorter version of the *pennon.* If you are of Scottish descent, remember that pinsils in Scotland are granted only to peers and barons.

PER: In the direction of.

PETASUS (PET-asus): A *morion* with wings, in the style of Mercury's hat.

PHOENIX (FEE-nix): The Egyptian mythological bird that rises from its own ashes. It is generally depicted as a *demi-eagle* with its wings outspread and, appropriately, rising up from flames. See Index.

PIERCED: Having a hole through which the *tincture* of the *field* can be seen. The hole is always circular unless *blazoned* otherwise. If a tincture that is not of the field is to be seen, this must be stated.

PIKE: A simple word that can cause confusion in heraldry. If you mean the fish, you should use the term *lucy.* If you mean the old infantry weapon you should probably use *spear.* If you mean the toll-gate on a turnpike, you are designing bad heraldry.

PILE: One of the *ordinaries.* It can be drawn in various ways but, typically, it is a triangle with its base along the top of the *shield* and its apex reaching to the approximate center of the shield. Piles that are reversed—i.e., with the base at the bottom of the shield—are *blazoned reversed* or *transposed.* They may also come from the sides in which case they are blazoned *dexter* or *sinister.* Several piles may be placed side by side but more than three begin to crowd the shield and can resemble a row of teeth. See Figure 4.

PILY: Said of a *field* or area divided by *piles* that are connected. This is occasionally *blazoned* "pily *counter* pily."

PILY BENDY: Similar to *pily*, but the resulting wedges are at an angle diagonally across the *field*.

PINEAPPLE: This term applies, oddly, to both the pine cone and the tropical fruit. It may be advisable to be specific in the *blazon*.

PINIONED: A synonym for *winged*.

PLANETS: See *symbols*.

PLATE: A silver *roundel*.

PLATY, PLATTÉ: Strewn with *plates*.

PLENITUDE: See *moon*.

PLUME: The type and number of *feathers* should be specified in the *blazon*. Otherwise, it will probably be represented as several *ostrich* feathers. See *panache*.

POINTED: Said of a *cross* whose limbs come to a point.

POINTS OF THE SHIELD: Designations given to various sections of the *shield*, primarily for purposes of easy *blazoning*. See Figure 2.

POLEAX: A *battle ax* with a long haft.

POMEGRANATE: Depicted with the seeds showing through an opening in the skin.

POMEIS, POMEY: A green *roundel*.

POMMEL: The ball at the end of a *dagger* or *sword hilt*.

POPINJAY: See *parrot*.

PORT: An entranceway, usually to a *castle*.

PORTCULLIS: An important heraldic *charge* based on the sliding wood or iron grille that was suspended in a gateway and capable of being quickly lowered should the need to do so arise. The charge is typically represented as having four vertical bars ending in points with four horizontal bars riveted across them. Usually the upper corners have chains attached which run alongside and under the portcullis and end in rings.

PORTCULLIS PURSUIVANT: An English heraldic officer.

POTENTY: One of the *lines of partition*. See Figure 6.

POWDERED, POUDRÉ: See *semy*.

PREYING: Describing a creature eating its prey; birds are sometimes described as "trussing."

PRIDE: See *peacock*.

PROBOSCIS: An elephant's trunk.

PROPER: If you want a *charge* to be drawn or painted essentially as it appears in real life, it must be *blazoned proper*, as "a book proper." (See Frontispiece.) It is sometimes abbreviated ppr.

PURPURE: The color purple; abbreviated purp.

PYTHON: Unless *blazoned proper,* a winged *serpent.*

QUARTER: An *ordinary* occupying one quarter—usually the *dexter chief* quarter, unless otherwise *blazoned*—of the *shield.* Actually, it is a large *canton.* When the shield is divided *per cross,* each division is a quarter.

QUARTERLY: Divided *per cross.* Reading from left to right, top to bottom, the quarters may be numbered when necessary: the *dexter chief* is the first quarter, the *sinister chief* is the second, etc.

QUARTERING: A method of combining two or more coats of *arms* into a single one. See Index.

QUATREFOIL (KWOT'r-foil, KAT'r-foil) : A flowerlike figure with four petals or leaves.

QUEUE (CUE) : A creature's tail.

QUEUED (CUED) : Having a tail.

FIG. 26.
Double-queued
Lion Rampant

QUEUE FOURCHY, FOURCHÉ (CUE FOOR-shay) : A forked tail. It is not the same as "doubled-queued," which means two separate tails. Queue fourchy indicates that the tail splits about a quarter of the way from the end.

QUILLED: See *ostrich.*

QUISE, À LA (AH LA KEES): Describing a bird's leg that is *erased* or *couped* at the thigh.

RABBIT: See *coney.*

RADIATED: See *irradiated.*

RAGULY, RAGULÉ (ruh-GOO-lee, RAG-ooly): One of the *lines of partition.* See Figure 6.

RAINBOW: Usually shown as a semicircle with its ends in *clouds.* (It is probably wise to include the clouds in the *blazon,* however, if they are wanted.)

RAM: An animal that has enjoyed some popularity in heraldry.

RAMPANT (RAM-pint): The most popular position for heraldic animals. The creature is shown upright with the left hind leg on the (often invisible) ground, and its other legs waving about. Unless otherwise *blazoned,* the creature faces the *dexter* side. See Figure 27.

FIG. 27.
Rampant

RAPIER: A long, thin, double-edged *sword.*

RAVEN: This bird should be colored black, of course. In Middle English, the raven was called a *corbie* and is often so *blazoned.*

RAYONNY, RAYONNÉ: One of the *lines of partition.* See Figure 6.

REBUS (REE-bis): A word, phrase or name represented by pictures. See Index and *canting arms.*

REFLECTED, REFLEXED: Bent or carried backward, as when a chain attached to a *collar* is "reflected" over the creature's back.

REGARDING: See *respectant.*

REGUARDANT, REGARDANT (re-GARD-int): Looking back over the shoulder. See Figure 28.

FIG. 28.
Rampant
reguardant

REINDEER: See *deer*.

RESPECTANT: Describing two creatures face to face. Synonyms are "aspectant," "regarding," "respecting," and "encoutrant." Also see *combatant*.

REVERSED: Upside-down. A "*pile* reversed," for example, emanates from the *base* of the *shield* rather than from the *chief*. Also "subverted" and "renverse."

RIBAND: An old-fashioned spelling for "ribbon" (which is also sometimes used). It is a diminutive of the *bend* and is narrower than the *bendlet*.

RICHMOND HERALD: An English heraldic officer.

RINGED: Having a ring, as at the end of a rope, leash, cord or *chain*.

RISING: Said of a bird with its wings spread as though it is about to take off.

ROACH: A name applied to various fishes of the carp family. If your artist lives in a city apartment or is known to smoke nontobacco substances, there may be some confusion unless your *blazon* specifies the kind of roach you have in mind.

ROCK: A rock may appear as a *compartment*, at the base of a *shield*, and even as part of the *crest*. If it is *blazoned proper*, it is painted gray.

ROLL OF ARMS: A scroll or book that is a record of coats of arms. See Index.

ROMPU: Interrupted or broken. A "*chevron* rompu" has the middle section placed above the two rising sides to give a broken effect.

Rook: In heraldry this always means the bird. The *blazon* should specify *chessrook* if that is what is intended.

Rose: Unless otherwise specified, the heraldic rose consists of five petals, with the seeds in the center and sepals between the petals. If *blazoned "barbed* and *seeded proper,"* the sepals are painted green and the seeds gold. The Tudor rose is a white rose superimposed over a red one. Obviously it is identified with the English Royal House of Tudor and represents the houses of Lancaster and York (hence, the War of the Roses). It is probably best to avoid using the Tudor rose in assumed *arms* unless there is a valid genealogical connection. If a more realistic rose is wanted, the blazon should specify the particular variety and perhaps include the term *proper* as well as the type to be used. The rose is the mark of *cadency* for the seventh son.

Rouge Croix Pursuivant: One of the English heraldic officers.

Rouge Dragon Pursuivant: One of the English heraldic officers.

Roundel, Roundle: A disc. This is a simple *charge* which, in my opinion, has become unnecessarily complicated. Roundels have been given different names: bezant, gold; plate, silver; torteau, red; pomey, green; pellet, gunstone, or ogress, black; golpe, purple. A fountain, wavy bands alternating white and blue (*barry wavy Argent* and *Azure*). See Figure 29.

FIG. 29.
Roundels

Rousant: See *rising*.

Rowel: The business end of a *spur*.

Rudder: Although not a historically popular *charge*, it can certainly be used these days in the *arms* of those with maritime associations or inclinations, or for *canting arms*.

Rustre: A *lozenge* with a round hole in the center.

Sable: Black; abbreviated s. or sa.

Sagittarius, Sagittary The *zodiac* sign. See *centaur* and Index.

Salamander: Heraldically, this unassuming little lizard has taken several forms, usually involving fire. Most frequently it is shown surrounded by flames and has even been depicted as a lion-tailed dog breathing fire. It is probably best to *blazon* it *proper* if that is what you intend.

Salient (SAIL-yint): Describing a creature that is leaping or springing. *Horses,* however, are *forcene; deer* are described as *springing*.

Salmon: The fish.

Saltire (SAWL-teer): One of the *ordinaries;* it is a *cross* placed on a *shield* to resemble the letter X. See Figure 4.

Saltirewise, Saltireways: In the direction of a *saltire;* "in saltire" is a synonym.

Sangliant, Sanglant: Blood-stained.

Sanguine (SANG-win): Blood color. This is one of the *stains* and is usually a somewhat deeper tone than *Gules*.

Sans: A French word meaning "without." It is used to describe a *charge* with something missing such as "a *ram* sans horns."

Sans Nombre: Without number; used when the *charge* is of a type where the quantity is left to the artist. See *semy*.

Saturn: The Roman god of agriculture and the sixth planet from the sun. The *blazon* should specify which meaning is intended.

Satyr (SAT-ur): From Greek mythology, a creature with the upper body of a man and the lower body of a *goat*. It is frequently associated with lechery and is an acceptable, if perhaps self-serving, *charge*. See *siren*.

Savage, Savageman: Usually shown bearded, with long hair, wreaths of leaves on his head and loins, and carrying a club.

Scales: See *balance*.

SCALING LADDER: Once an important military appliance used for climbing the enemy's fortified walls. It is usually shown with two or three upright supports topped by hooks.

SCALLOP: See *escallop*.

SCEPTRE: A batonlike emblem of office. If used as a *charge*, it is best to specify the office.

SCIMITAR, SCYMETAR, SCIMETAR (SIM-ittar): A short, curved *sword*, broad at the point and tapering toward the handle; frequently associated with Persians and Turks. See *falchion* and *seax*.

SCORPIO, SCORPION: The first is the *zodiac* sign; the second is the arachnid.

SCRIP, SCRIPT: A pouch or purse used by pilgrims; often shown hanging from a *bourdon*, although it can be a separate *charge*. The *blazon* usually refers to it as a "palmer's script."

SEA: Even if a *blazon* specifies "waves of the sea proper," the artist may show a realistic-looking ocean or use the alternating wavy white and blue stripes (*"barry wavy Argent and Azure"*).

SEA-: With the exception of "dog" and "wolf," the prefix *sea*- refers to a creature whose top half is as specified and whose lower portions of those of a fish. Thus, there are sea-dragons, sea-stags, etc. This can sometimes cause trouble when the compound word refers to a real creature. Unless you specify "sea-lion *proper*," you will come up not with a member of the seal family, but with a fishy-tailed *lion*. The same is true for sea-horse. If you mean the real thing, you should specify *hippocampus*.

SEA-DOG: A *talbot* with the tail of an *otter*, webbed feet, a dorsal fin and scales.

SEA-WOLF: A *wolf* with the same aquatic accessories as the sea-dog.

SEAX (SAY-ax): A *sword* resembling a *scimitar* but with a notch on the back behind the point. It was used by the Saxons. See *falchion*.

SEEDED: Used to describe the seeds of a flower. See *rose*.

SEGREANT (SEG-riant): A synonym for *rampant* when referring to a *dragon* or *griffin*.

Sᴇᴊᴀɴᴛ, Sᴇᴊᴇᴀɴᴛ (SEE-jint): Describing a creature that is sitting down and with four paws on the ground. It faces to the *dexter* unless otherwise *blazoned*. The position of the head must also be indicated. See *squirrel*.

FIG. 30.
Semy of fleur-de-lis
(or, semy de lis)

Sᴇᴍʏ, Sᴇᴍᴇ́ (SEM-mee): Scattered or strewn with an unspecified number of small *charges*. The suffix "-y" after a charge indicates a semy of that charge. For example, "besanty" is equivalent to "a semy of besants." Synonyms for semy are: "powdered," "poudré," "strewn," "strewed," "aspersed," and "replenished." See Figure 30.

Sᴇʀᴘᴇɴᴛ: Almost any artistic rendition of a non-specific snake will do, unless a particular kind is specified. Serpents are usually shown *nowed* or *encircled,* so any other position should be indicated.

Sʜᴀᴄᴋʟᴇ Bᴏʟᴛ, Sʜᴀᴄᴋʙᴏʟᴛ: A manacle of the simplest kind; it is U-shaped with rings at the two ends, through which is passed a cylindrical bar. See *fetterlock.*

Sʜᴀғᴛᴇᴅ: Used to describe the shaft of an *arrow* or *spear* when specifying its *tincture,* e.g., "shafted *sable.*"

Sʜᴀᴋᴇғᴏʀᴋ: A Y-shaped *charge* that looks like a *pall* except that it is *couped,* i.e., cut off at the ends with points conforming to the corners of the *shield.*

Sʜᴀᴍʀᴏᴄᴋ: Unless *blazoned proper,* this will probably be drawn as a *trefoil* with broad, scalloped leaves and *slipped.*

SHANK: The upright section of an *anchor*.

SHEAF: This refers to a bundle of *arrows*. (The proper term for a bundle of grain is *garb*.)

SHEEP: Typically, heraldic sheep are *blazoned Agnus Dei* or *fleece*. These *charges* may be used, or you may specify "a sheep *proper*," and indicate its posture and position.

SHELLS: The specific type must be indicated in the *blazon*. The most common found in heraldry is the *escallop*.

SHIELD: The form or pattern on which the vast majority of coats of *arms* are displayed. See Chapter 14 and Index.

SHIELD OF DAVID: See *David, Shield of*.

SHIP: Many kinds of ships appear in heraldry, and the specific type must be given in the *blazon*, complete with details as to whether sails (if any) are unfurled and where and how flags and *pennons* are to be placed. In heraldry, a ship sails to the *dexter* unless otherwise blazoned. See *lymphad*.

SHUTTLE, SHUTTLE COCK: The weaver's tool, used for carrying the threads of the woof between those of the warp. It appears in the *canting arms* of Shuttleworth and is, of course, a good *charge* for occupational references.

SINISTER: The word means "left," but in heraldry it refers to the point of view of the individual carrying the *shield;* therefore, to the observer, it is the right-hand side of the shield. See *dexter* and Index.

SIREN: In Greek mythology, a creature who led sailors to their deaths. She is often incorrectly shown as a *mermaid*. The heraldic siren has the head and torso of a woman; the lower portions are those of a sea-bird with webbed feet and enormous wings. Today, the word describes a fascinating, but ultimately treacherous, woman. A coat of *arms* displaying a siren and a *satyr* could present a family image that would allow for considerable interesting speculation.

SIXFOIL: A flowerlike *charge* with six petals.

SLIP: A twig bearing two or three leaves. See *sprig*.

SLIPPED: Used when flowers or leaves are to be shown having stalks.

SNAKE: See *serpent*.

SNOWFLAKE: It was not until the twentieth century that snowflakes were used as *charges*. Aesthetically, they are very appealing. The strictly correct *blazon* is "snow crystals" and the star-shaped forms are used.

SOARING: Flying.

SOMERSET HERALD: An English heraldic officer.

SOUTHERN CROSS: The constellation. It is depicted with five stars (*mullets*)—one with eight points, two with seven, and one each with six and five points. The *blazon* is "a representation of the Southern Cross."

SPADE: The implement. The playing-card suit is not considered good heraldry. However, see *heart*.

SPANCELLED: Describing a *horse* with a foreleg and a hind leg held by *fetterlocks*.

SPEAR: Unless otherwise specified, the tilting spear—that is, the kind used in medieval tournaments—is shown. Any other kind, such as a tribal spear, should be specifically *blazoned*.

SPHERE: See *armillary sphere, terrestrial globe*.

SPHINX: Heraldically shown with the head and breasts of a woman and the body of a *lion,* sometimes with wings. The head is covered with the traditional Egyptian headdress. The position is usually *couchant* unless otherwise specified.

SPIDER: This *charge* shows up in existing heraldry and is perfectly acceptable. If a *field* is charged with a spider's web, the center of the web is usually at the center (i.e., the *fess point*), from which the web radiates.

SPRIG: A small branch or twig bearing five or six leaves. See *slip*.

SPRINGING: *Salient* when referring to *deer*.

SPUR: A commonly used heraldic *charge* always shown with a *rowel* and placed upright with the rowel on top. If some other type of spur or position is desired the *blazon* must so specify.

SQUARE: See *carpenter's square*.

SQUIRREL: Always drawn *sejant erect,* i.e., sitting upright, unless otherwise *blazoned*. It is often shown holding a nut in its forepaws.

STAG: See *deer*.

STAINS: *Murrey, Sanguine,* and *Tenné* are often called stains, perhaps to differentiate them from the more frequently used *colors*. Traditionally, they were used in *abatements,* which were regarded as a "stain" on a coat of arms.

STALKED: See *leaf*.

STAR: See *estoil, mullet*.

STATANT (STAY-tint): Describing creatures standing on all fours. See Figure 31.

FIG. 31.
Statant

STEPS: See *degrees*.

STIRRUP: Be specific in the *blazon;* indicate whether the leather is to be shown or only the stirrup iron.

STOCK: A *tree* stump.

STORK: See *heron*.

STREWED, STREWN: See *semy,* which is the preferred term.

STRINGED: Used when the strings of an instrument, a bow, or any other kind of string is of a *tincture* different from whatever it is attached to.

SUBORDINARIES: See *ordinaries*.

SUBVERTED: See *reversed*.

SUFFLUE: See *clarion*.

SUN: Unless very specifically *blazoned* to the contrary, the sun is always shown with long, wedge-shaped rays that are alternately straight and wavy, and with a human face. It is typically blazoned as "a sun in his splendor" or, less frequently, as "a sun in his glory."

SUNBURST: The *sun's* rays emanating from *clouds*.

SUPPORTERS: Figures used to hold up a *shield*. See Figure 1 and Index.

SURMOUNTED: See *debruised*.

SWALLOW: The bird.

SWAN: An attractive and versatile *charge*.

SWASTIKA: In heraldry, a form of *cross* (see Figure 11). A once time-honored symbol of many cultures, it is now in disrepute because of its associations with Nazis.

SWORD: The long, straight-bladed variety with a crosspiece and grip, at the end of which is a *pommel*. There is, however, a wide variety of swords, and if one of these is intended, the details should be given in the *blazon*. (For example, see *scimitar, seax.*)

SYMBOLS: A wide variety of symbols, drawing on almost any profession, can be used in modern heraldry. See Index.

TALBOT: Heraldry's most popular *dog*. It is depicted with the head of a hound, the ears of a bloodhound, and the body of a mastiff.

TASSELLED: Having tassels, a frequent adornment for *cushions*.

TENNÉ, TENNY: A darkish orange. Also "tawny," "busk" or, more simply, "orange." One of the *stains*.

TENT: Usually, this is shown as a circular tent with open flaps through which the center pole can be seen. Other types are sometimes *blazoned* as *pavilions*. See Index.

TERRESTRIAL GLOBE: A representation of the earth with some indications of longitudinal and latitudinal lines and land masses.

THISTLE: An obviously popular *charge* in Scottish heraldry; usually shown *slipped* and leaved.

THROUGHOUT: See *entire*.

THUNDERBOLT: In heraldry this consists of an entwined column of flames between wings with four jagged bolts of lightning *in saltire*, i.e., X-shaped. Any other kind of thunderbolt should be very carefully *blazoned*.

TIARA: The papal crown; not jewelry.

TIERCED: Divided into three sections. As an example, see Frontispiece, which is blazoned as *tierced per pall reversed*.

TIGER: To be used when describing the striped beast; it should be *blazoned* "a tiger *proper*." See *Tyger*.

TILTING SPEAR: See *spear*.

TINCTURES: Heraldic *colors, metals*, and *furs*. See Index.

TORCH: The classical cone-shaped torch with flames coming out of the top is typically *blazoned* a "torch enflamed."

TORQUED: Having a *wreath*.

TORSE: The twisted material out of which the *crest* rises. See Index and *wreath*.

TORTEAU (tor-TOE): A red *roundel*.

TOURNÉ: Synonym for *contourné*.

TOWER: A tower with battlements, with a bricklike pattern overall. It is usually shown with a port or opening at the base, and sometimes has turrets at the top, in which case the number should be indicated.

TRANSFIXED, TRANSPIERCED: *Pierced* through as with an *arrow*. Compare *pierced*.

TRANSFLUENT: Used to describe flowing *water*, usually under a *bridge*.

TREE: Any identifiable tree is a legitimate *charge* as long as it is specified in the *blazon*. See *eradicated*.

TREFLÉ: Strewn with *trefoils*.

TREFOIL: A flowerlike figure with three petals. See *shamrock*.

TRESSURE: A narrower version of the *orle*, often shown double and *blazoned* "double tressure."

TRIANGLE: Always an equilateral triangle unless otherwise specified. See *David, Shield of*.

TRICK, TRICKING: Technique for indicating the *tinctures* of a coat of *arms*. See Index.

TRICORPORATE: Having three bodies emanating from one head.

TRIDENT: The three-pronged, pitchfork-like *spear* usually associated with *Neptune*.

TRIPARTED, TRIPARTITE: Synonyms for *tierced*.

TRIPPANT: A synonym for *passant;* used to describe various *deer*.

TRITON: The mythical figure frequently associated with maritime activities; also the nucleus of tritium. See Index.

TRUMPET: Heraldically, a long, straight horn tapering out at the bell; any other kind has to be specified. See *bugle horn*.

TRUSSED: Used to describe a creature with wings closed.

TRUSSING: Said of a bird that is devouring its prey.

TUDOR ROSE: See *rose*.

TUFTED: Used to describe the tufts of hair on creatures' limbs, tails, etc. when their *tincture* is different from that of the body. See *crined*.

TUN: A large cask or barrel, frequently used for wine; an overworked but nevertheless useful *rebus* for people whose names end in "ton."

TURKEY: A very American *charge,* frequently *blazoned* "in his pride"; i.e., with tail outspread.

TURRET: See *tower*.

TWYFOIL: See *unifoil*.

TYGER: A zoological mishmash. It has the body of a *lion*, pointed ears, a kind of beak at the end of its nose, tusks, and tufts of hair on its paws. If this is the beast you want, use the ancient spelling given here. See *tiger*.

TYNES, TINES: The points on the *antlers* of a stag.

UMBRATED: See *adumbration*.

UNDY, UNDÉ, ONDÉ: A synonym for *wavy*.

UNGULED: See *hoofed*.

UNICORN: A very popular and highly symbolic heraldic creature, usually shown as a *horse* with a long, twisted horn coming from its forehead, the legs and cloven hooves of a stag, and the tail of a *lion*. See Index.

UNICORN PURSUIVANT: A Scottish heraldic officer.

UNIFOIL: Although this *charge* is described as resembling one of the leaves of the traditional flowerlike "foil," it does not seem to actually exist. The same is true of the twyfoil, which is supposed to have two leaves or petals.

URCHIN, URCHEON: See *hedgehog*.

URDY: One of the *lines of partition*. See Figure 6.

URIANT, URINANT: Describing a fish with its head down and, unless otherwise specified, its belly to the *sinister*.

URINAL: Apparently, this *charge* occurs only once in English heraldry and is *blazoned* "an urinal in its cage proper." it is drawn as a decanter inside a cagelike, straight-sided bucket with a rope handle. If you are a plumber dedicated to your craft, you may want to use this charge. Any other version is unacceptable, to say the least.

URSA MAJOR: The constellation. See Index.

VAIR: One of the two main heraldic *furs*. See Index.

VAIRY, VAIRÉ: Having the pattern of *vair*, but of other *tinctures*, which, of course, must be specified in the *blazon*.

VAMBRACED: Used to describe an *arm* covered with armor.

VAMPLATE: The hand guard on a tilting *spear*.

VANE: For practical purposes, this should refer to a weather vane, but it is also sometimes a synonym for *fan* and is a type of small flag. It is best to be specific.

VEINED: Used to describe the veins of a *leaf* when their *tincture* is not the same as that of the leaf itself. It is a synonym for *nerved* and is more frequently used.

VERDÉ, VERDOY: Strewn (*semy*) with plants or leaves.

VERT (vurt): The color green; abbreviated v. or vt.

VESTED: A synonym for *habited*.

VIROLS, VIROLLES, VEROLLES: The bands around a horn. See *bugle horn*.

VOIDED: Used to describe a *charge* that has had its middle removed, leaving not much more than the outline and allowing the *tincture* of the *field* or another tincture to show through.

VOLANT: Describing a bird in flight. It is usually shown with its legs drawn up (to differentiate it from a bird *rising*) and, unless otherwise *blazoned,* faces the *dexter* side.

VOLUTED: A synonym for *encircled,* when describing *serpents.*

VORANT: Devouring.

VULNED: Describing a creature that has been wounded and is bleeding. If it has been vulned with a *sword, dagger,* etc., the weapon is shown sticking into the body. If it pierces the body, the *blazon* should specify "pierced" or *transfixed,* followed by the object. See *pelican.*

WATER: Even though the *blazon* may specify "water *proper,*" you may still wind up with the symbolic version. In most cases, however, that is the more attractive form, anyway. It is blazoned *water barry wavy Argent* and *Azure,* wavy bands alternating white and blue. The number of bands may be indicated. "Waves of the sea" stands a better chance of being drawn naturally.

WATER-BOUGET, WATER BUDGET: See *bouget.*

WATTLED: A synonym for *jelloped.*

WAVY: One of the *lines of partition;* a wavy line. See Figure 6.

WEATHER VANE: See *vane.*

WELL: It is best to be specific in the *blazon.* Typically, wells not described in detail are shown as cylindrical masonry structures seen from slightly above.

WHEAT: Single stalks or a specific number of stalks may be used. See *garb.*

WHEEL: A cartwheel with eight spokes is common. Any other kind should be *blazoned.* See *Catherine wheel.*

WHELK: See *shell.*

WHIRLPOOL: See *gurges*.

WILDMAN: See *savage* and *wodehouse*.

WINDSOR HERALD: An English heraldic officer. The title dates back to the mid-fourteenth century.

WINGED: In heraldry, wings can be attached to virtually anything.

WINNOWING FAN: See *fan*.

WODEHOUSE, WOODHOUSE: An obvious *charge* for *canting arms,* it requires supreme self-confidence on the part of the bearer. It is a bearded "wild man of the woods," covered with green hair, except for the face, elbows, knees, hands, and feet.

WREATH: British heraldists seem to prefer this word to *torse*. However, *charges* may be "wreathed," that is, encircled by a garland of flowers or some other device. It will probably avoid confusion, therefore, if "wreath" is used for anything other than the torse.

WYVERN, WIVERN, WYVER: A heraldic beast that looks exactly like a *dragon* except that instead of "normal" hindquarters it has the rear end of a *serpent* ending in a *barbed* tail.

YALE: A rather queer monster best left alone. Its main features are long tusks and long, curved horns that it can swivel. It has been shown as a kind of *antelope* with the tail of a *lion,* and elsewhere as a rather heavier animal with the tail of a *goat*.

YORK HERALD: An English heraldic officer.

ZODIAC, SIGNS OF THE: The signs of the Zodiac can be *blazoned* in their pictorial representation, as constellations, or as astronomical symbols. Overall design and purpose are likely to dictate which.

12

Heraldic Organizations

A few minutes' time at your local library or chamber of commerce will provide you with the names of genealogical and historical societies that may be able to assist you in conducting searches. There is one for every state in the union, and there are many regional, county and city historical societies, even in some relatively small municipalities.

Virtually every one of these organizations will also be able to assist you in locating a genealogist and, most likely, a heraldist and a heraldic artist.

If your ancestors covered considerable territory in their travels and settlements, you may require the services of more than one organization. Excellent detailed lists by state and region are available. (See Bibliography.)

The organizations listed below are concerned primarily with the heraldry of the countries in which they exist. Many are private groups of individuals with an interest in both the historical and artistic aspects of heraldry, and, while the information given in this section is as accurate as possible at the time of publication, it should be remembered that because they *are* private groups, interests and priorities of named individuals may have changed by the time you read this.

AUSTRALIA
The Heraldry Society of Australia
c/o Col. A. G. Puttock
19 Haverbrack Avenue
Malvern, S.E. 4, Victoria

AUSTRIA
Adler Society
Haarhof 4a,
Vienna 1

BELGIUM
For information on genealogy and heraldry write to:
Office Généalogique et Héraldique de Belgique
Museés Royaux d'Art et d'Histoire
10 Parc du Cinquantenaire
B-1040 Brussels

If you believe one of your ancestors held a noble title or was armigerous, write to:
Le Conseil Héraldique
85 rue du Prince Royal
Brussels

CANADA
The Heraldry Society of Canada
c/o Mr. Norman A. Nunn
900 Pinecrest Road
Ottawa 14, Ontario

CENTRAL, SOUTH AMERICA
Central and South American heraldry is derived primarily from Spanish and, to a somewhat lesser extent, Portuguese heraldry. There are also French and English influences. For investigations into Central and South American ancestral heraldry, therefore, it is probably best to go directly to the European sources.

DENMARK
For information about ancient coats of arms, write to:
National Archives
Rigsarkivet
9 Rigsdagsgarden, DK 1218
Copenhagen, K

For general heraldic information covering not only Denmark but the rest of Scandinavia, write to:
Dr. Ole Rostock, Secretary
Heraldisk Selskab
Sigmundsvej 8
2880 Bagsvaerd

ENGLAND, WALES, NORTHERN IRELAND
If you believe you are entitled to a coat of arms borne by an ancestor, or if you want a coat of arms granted to you by virtue of English, Welsh or Northern Irish ancestry, write to:
Secretary to the Earl Marshal
The College of Arms
Queen Victoria Street
London, EC4V 4BT

For assistance—for a fee—in conducting genealogical research and/or designing a coat of arms, there are few better than:
Achievements Ltd.
Northgate
Canterbury, Kent CT1 1BA, England

This estimable establishment is presided over by the knowledgeable and expert C. A. Humphery-Smith, one of the moving forces of the Heraldry Society.

The Society may be able to provide the names of other individuals ready to assist you. It can also contribute significantly to your own interest in heraldry, not only in Britain but internationally. They publish a newsletter and a quarterly magazine. Write to:
Secretary, The Heraldry Society
28 Museum Street
London, WC1 1LH
(See separate listing for SCOTLAND.)

FINLAND

If you believe you are descended from Finnish nobility, heraldic information should be available from:
House of the Nobility
Riddarhusgenealogen
Riddarhuset
Helsinki

The Heraldiske Selskab, listed under Denmark, covers Finnish heraldry. The organization that deals solely with Finnish heraldry is:
Suomen Heraldinen Seura
c/o Olof Eriksson
Gravlingsvagen 6 D 57
Hertonas

FRANCE

A roll of arms containing some 40,000 coats, known as the *Grand Armorial,* is published by:
Societé du Grand Armorial de France
179 Boulevard Haussmann
Paris

The French heraldic society is:
Societé Française d'Héraldique et de Sigillographie
113 rue de Courcelles
Paris 17

GERMANY (West)

If you believe you are entitled, by inheritance, to a German coat of arms, write to:
Der Herold
Verein fur Heraldik
Archivstr. 12–14
1000 Berlin 33

Other heraldic organizations are:
Wappen-Herold
Tharandterstr. 2
1 Berlin 31

Zum Kleeblatt
Forbacherstr. 8
Hannover-Kirchrode

IRISH REPUBLIC
A good deal of Irish heraldry is recorded in various English
archives, including the College of Arms. Since 1943 the Irish
Republic has had an official herald. If you believe that you have an
armigerous ancestor, or you can prove that you are descended from
or related to an Irish clan chief, write to:
The Chief Herald of Ireland
Dublin Castle
Dublin 2
(For Northern Ireland, see ENGLAND.)

ITALY
Although there is no official regulating body in Italy, there is a col-
lege of arms, of sorts. If you believe that you are descended from
Italian nobility, write to:
Collegio Araldico
16 Via Santa Maria dell'Anima
Rome

For general questions and information on Italian heraldry and an-
cestry write to:
Istituto Italiano di Genealogia e Araldica
Palazzo della Scimmia
18 Via dei Portoghesi
Rome

NETHERLANDS
Koninklijk Nederlandsch Genootschap voor
Geslacht-en-Wapenkunde
Bleijenburg 5
The Hague

NORWAY
The Heraldisk Selskab, listed under Denmark, also has consid-

erable information and resources relating to Norwegian heraldry.
The Norwegian heraldic organization is:
Norsk Heraldisk Forening
c/o Hans A.K.T. Cappelen
Bygdoy Allé 123B
Oslo 2

If you think your Norwegian ancestry may have been armigerous,
write to:
Universitetsbiblioteket i Oslo
Drammensveien 42B
Oslo

POLAND
Chevalier Leonard J. Suligowski
Director of Heraldry
Polish Nobility Association
529 Dunkirk Road
Baltimore, MD 21212

PORTUGAL
In 1755 a ruinous earthquake destroyed most of the records of Portugal's coats of arms. The few that remain are on file at:
Arquivo Nacional da Torre do Tombo
Lisbon

The Portuguese heraldry organization is:
Instituto Portugues de Heraldica
Largo do Carmo
Lisbon 2

RUSSIA
Russian Nobility Association
971 First Avenue
New York, NY 10022

SCOTLAND
To obtain a legitimate coat of arms from Scotland you must either
prove descendance from an armigerous ancestor or prove that you
are of Scottish descent. In the latter case you may apply for a grant

of arms to your ancestor. When—and if—that is granted, you may then apply to have those arms reassigned to you. Details can be obtained by writing to:

Court of the Lord Lyon
Lyon Office, H.M. New Register House
Edinburgh EH1 3YT

SOUTH AMERICA (See CENTRAL AMERICA)

SOUTH AFRICA

The Heraldry Society of Southern Africa
Postbox 4839
Cape Town

SPAIN

By the end of the eighteenth century there were some half-million *hidalgos* (noblemen) in Spain, every one of them armigerous. Given their proliferation and their propensity for colonization, their descendants are probably all over the globe. If you think you are the descendant of an *hidalgo*, you may be able to get verification from:

Asociación de Hidalgos
Calle de Atocha 94
Madrid

Spain has an official heraldic officer who is authorized to grant arms to Spanish citizens, descendants of Spanish citizens, and residents of former Spanish colonies. If you fall into any of these categories and want a formal grant of arms, apply to:

Cronista Rey de Armas
Dirección y Administración
Calle de Atocha 91
Madrid

Additional information on Spanish genealogy and heraldry may be obtained from:

Instituto Internacional de Genealogia y Heraldica
Calle de Atocha 94
Madrid

SWEDEN
Heraldiske Selskab, listed under Denmark, can offer information on Swedish heraldry. If you have affiliations with Swedish nobility, you may be able to obtain an approval of a coat of arms, or information about ancestral coats of arms, from:
    Riksheraldiker
    Riddarhuset
    P. O. Box 2022,
    S-103 11, Stockholm

There is also a Swedish heraldry society:
    Vastra Sveriges Heraldiska Sallskap
    c/o Leif Pahlsson
    Frotroligheten 4
    412 70 Gothenburg

UNITED STATES
If you want assistance in tracing possible armigerous connections, or in having a coat of arms devised for you, contact:
    The Augustin Society
    1617 West 261st Street
    Harbor City, CA 90710

If you believe you are of royal British lineage, swallow your pride and write to:
    Descendants of the Illegitimate Sons and Daughters of the Kings of Britain
    c/o Brainer T. Peck
    Lakeside, CT 06758

WALES (See ENGLAND)

13

Charges

On the following pages is a selection of some of the more commonly used charges in heraldry. The fact that they are popular should not deter you from using them freely; the likelihood of your coming up with a combination of charges, tinctures, and placement that exactly duplicates someone else's coat of arms is extremely slim—unless you devise one with only one or two charges.

A mathematician probably could, given a little time and a large computer, calculate the many hundreds, even thousands, of variations for each charge, resulting from available tinctures, poses, and positions. It is important to remember that the position or pose in which a charge is depicted is not the only one you can use; a lion may be shown *rampant* here, but in your coat of arms it can be shown *couchant, sejant, guardant, regardant,* or in any of the other poses in which other beasts are depicted. The same is true, of course, for any other creature you choose—including those not shown here.

Do try, however, to retain some sense of reason, even if your charge is fanciful. You could, presumably, blazon a coat of arms with *a camel's head affronty,* but I pity the artist who would be commissioned to render it, and I suspect that no matter how expert the artwork, most viewers would have difficulty recognizing it. Why do it, when *a camel statant* renders a clear and unmistakable profile?

Also keep in mind that only a minuscule sampling of all the

FIG. 32. Charges

1. Agnus Dei

2. Antelope

Statant

3. Arm

Arm embowed

4. Arm

Cubit Arm

5. Bears

Addorsed

6. Bee

Volant proper

7. Boar's Head

Caboshed

8. Castle

9. Chess Rook

10. Cinquefoil

11. Crane

In its vigilance

12. Crescent

13. Deer

At gaze (guardant)

14. Dolphin

Embowed

15. Eagle

Close

16. Eagle

Displayed

17. Eagle

Double-headed

18. Eagle

19. Falcon

·Belled and jessed

20. Fleur-de-lis

21. Fox's Head

Erased

22. Garb

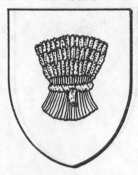

23. Griffin

Segreant

24. Griffins

Combatant

25. Hand

Hand appaumé

26. Martlets

27. Mermaid

28. Oak

Fructed

29. Owl

46. Unicorn

Passant

47. Wings

Conjoined in lure

48. Wyvern

Erect

charges that have appeared in heraldry is offered here, and that you have at your disposal charges that have never been used. Your resources are literally unlimited. Let appropriateness, good sense, and good taste be your guides.

41. Trefoil

Stalked, slipped

42. Triton

43. Tyger

Sejant

44. Tyger

Sejant erect

45. Tyger

Sejant affronty

35. Rose

Barbed and seeded

36. Rose

Slipped and leaved

37. Sea Horses

Respectant

38. Sea Lion

Reguardant

39. Sun

In splendor

40. Talbot's Head

Couped

30. Pegasus

Courant, collared

31. Pelican

In her piety

32. Phoenix

33. Pike

Naiant

34. Portcullis

14

Coat-of-Arms Blanks

The following pages contain several blank forms consisting of model armorial achievements: shield, helmet, torse, and mantling. If you require the augmentations of crests, supporters, or additional helmets, you will have to assemble them yourself. That can easily be done by simply drawing them in or by adopting or adapting the charges shown in Chapter 13 and elsewhere throughout the book.

You may want to consider making your initial efforts on tracing paper or on Xerox copies of these outlines.

When you are ready to commit your design more-or-less permanently, try to do so in color; a child's crayons will serve admirably. If, however, you lack the resources or inclination for colorwork, remember to use *hatching* or *tricking* to designate the various tinctures.

One more point before you begin work: This is supposed to be fun. Enjoy yourself.

Notes

With three exceptions, all of the notes refer to works that are listed alphabetically by author in the Bibliography. The references below, therefore, are to authors' names.

1. Mackinnon
2. Gibbon
3. Scott-Giles (*Motley*)
4. Koch
5. Scott-Giles (*Motley*)
6. *The Heraldry Gazette*, No. 73, May 1978: The Heraldry Society, London
7. Bardsley
8. Kaganoff
9. *Ibid.*
10. Bardsley
11. Dennys
12. Boutell
13. Neubecker
14. *Ibid.*
15. *Ibid.*
16. von Volborth
17. Brooke-Little
18. *Ibid.*
19. Neubecker
20. White
21. *Ibid.*
22. Brooke-Little

23. *Ibid.*
24. Scott-Giles (*Motley*)
25. Boutell
26. Pine
27. von Volborth
28. *Ibid.*
29. Boutell
30. Stewart, John: "Every Man a Saint," *Saturday Review,* January 1980
31. Moncreiffe
32. Boutell
33. Dennys
34. *Ibid.*
35. von Volborth
36. Koch
37. Boutell
38. Sansweet, Stephen J.: "Mail-order Ancestors: Coat-of-Arms Sales Boom Irking Experts," *The Wall Street Journal,* June 5, 1969
39. Dennys
40. Neubecker
41. *Ibid.*

Bibliography

Any attempt to compile a bibliography of heraldic works on a country-by-country basis would probably require a volume equal to the size of the one you are now holding. Several of the books listed below contain such references; these are so indicated.

The books are listed alphabetically by author, rather than in order of importance. I have included some observations about most of the books listed. For those with a limited attention span, however, I will mention now that in my opinion, the most definitive work on heraldry is *Boutell's Heraldry;* the best book for do-it-yourself genealogy is *How to Find Your Family Roots.*

Some—but certainly not all—of the books listed should be available in large public libraries. Book dealers specializing in genealogy (easily located by checking your local classified telephone directory) may be able to supply you with some of the other titles, especially if you are willing to settle for secondhand copies. Dealers who specialize in locating wanted titles (also listed in the classified telephone directory) can be of invaluable assistance in obtaining the book you want. Many such dealers do not charge a fee for the search unless they find the book.

I have always found the best source for heraldic reference material to be Heraldry Today, in London. Presided over by Mrs. Rosemary Pinches, this establishment, something of a bookstore, but something more, too, has in its stock many of the standard works on heraldry as well as some that are not so standard. Those who have dealt with English book dealers can attest to the pleasure of doing business with them. Invariably, they are prompt, courteous, knowledgeable, trustworthy, and ready to help. Heraldry Today is the embodiment of all of these qualities. If Mrs. Pinches does not have a reference work relating to the national heraldry of your particular interest, chances are she knows where to find one. The firm publishes booklists containing currently available titles on heraldry and genealogy and will be glad to place you on their mailing list for the asking. Write to Heraldry Today, Parliament Piece, Ramsbury, Nr. Marlborough, Wiltshire, England. (If you visit London, you may be able to find the small but well-stocked shop at 10 Beauchamp [pronounced Beecham] Place, where Mrs. Pinches and her staff have held forth for years. At this writing, however, there were some problems with the lease.) When you write or visit, give her my regards.

ALLCOCK, HUBERT, *Heraldic Design* (New York: Tudor Publishing Co., 1962). This slim volume is crammed with excellent examples of coats of arms, numerous charges, and some basic details of heraldry. It will prove especially useful to the artist looking for good heraldic models.

BAIN, ROBERT, *The Clans and Tartans of Scotland* (London and Glasgow: William Collins Sons & Co., Ltd., 1973). This lovely little volume contains color plates of many Scottish tartans as well as the accompanying crest badges. First published in 1938, the edition referred to here is an enlarged and revised version.

BARDSLEY, CHARLES WAREING, *English Surnames: Their Sources and Significations* (Rutland, Vermont: Charles E. Tuttle Company, Inc.; London: Prentice-Hall International, Inc.; 1968). Except for a brief publisher's foreword, this is a facsimile of a book originally published in London in 1889. It covers the origins of thousands of names and is written in a simple yet elegant style.

BARBER, RICHARD, *The Knight and Chivalry* (London: Longman Group Limited, 1970). Probably everything you ever wanted to know about the subjects in the title.

BEARD, TIMOTHY FIELD, with DENISE DEMONG, *How to Find Your Family Roots* (New York: McGraw-Hill, 1977). For anyone interested in conducting a genealogical search, this thick volume is well worth its price. It is jam-packed with lists. Here you will find genealogical sources for every state and for almost every country, including those in Africa. About a quarter of the volume is devoted to methods and techniques for conducting the search. The chapter on heraldry, of necessity, does not go into very great depth, but then, it is not a heraldry book. Not incidentally, Mr. Beard is with the History and Genealogy Department of the New York Public Library, an institution well worth visiting if you are on a genealogical hunt.

BOUTELL: See Brooke-Little.

BROOKE-LITTLE, J. P., *An Heraldic Alphabet* (London: Macdonald and Company Publishers Limited, 1973). Mr. Brooke-Little is the Richmond Herald in the English College of Arms and is a recognized international expert on heraldry, particularly British heraldry. This well-illustrated little volume contains a short but comprehensive introduction to heraldry and, through the illustrations of the definitions, a wealth of charges that can be used.

BROOKE-LITTLE, J. P., *Boutell's Heraldry* (London and New York: Frederick Warne and Company Limited, 1970). In 1863 Reverend Charles Boutell published the first edition of *The Manual of Heraldry*. It has become a classic and has been updated and revised several times. This latest revision, by one of the most famous (and justly so) of heralds is, in effect, a readable textbook on heraldry. Its orientation is, understandably, principally British; nevertheless, if you use it as a point of reference, you cannot go wrong. If you decide to own only one major heraldry book, this should be the one.

DENNYS, RODNEY, *The Heraldic Imagination* (New York: Clarkson N. Potter, Inc., 1975). The author is the English Somerset Herald of Arms. This book could easily be dismissed as a "coffee table" showpiece, but it would be a mistake to do so. It is handsomely illustrated and filled with information, including a bibliography of nearly three dozen European and British medieval heraldic treatises, many with rolls of arms.

DIXON, JANICE T., and DORA D. FLACK, *Preserving Your Past* (Garden City: Doubleday & Company, Inc., 1977). This book is subtitled, "A Painless Guide to Writing Your Autobiography and Family History." It is. This is another major source of regional and ethnic genealogical and historical organizations.

DREYFUSS, HENRY, *Symbol Sourcebook* (New York: McGraw-Hill, 1972). It is impossible to imagine that such an important work could ever be out of print. The title is highly descriptive: the author has included international symbols of every kind, ranging from Accommodations and Travel, through Folklore and Home Economics, Medicine, Religion, Safety, and Traffic. The Table of Contents is in eighteen languages, including Swahili, Chinese, Arabic, Hebrew, and Hindi.

GIBBON, JOHN, *Introductio ad Latinam Blasoniam, an essay to a more correct BLASON in Latine than formerly hath been used*. This marvelous little book was first published in 1682. A limited paperback facsimile edition was published in 1962 by Achievements Limited, 58 Northgate, Canterbury, England. Despite its title, only the blazons are translated into Latin. The book is lavishly illustrated and includes such delightful passages as the author's comments on seeing American Indians doing a dance. Admittedly a piece of heraldic *curiosa,* if you can find a copy, it is worth having.

GIBBS-SMITH, CHARLES H., *The Bayeux Tapestry* (New York, London: Phaidon Publishers, 1973). A comprehensive and comprehensively illustrated study of the tapestry that is a document of the Norman Conquest of England.

KAGANOFF, BENZION C., *A Dictionary of Jewish Names and Their History* (New York: Schocken Books, 1977). In 1837, Leopold Zunz published a study of Jewish names. Since then, Rabbi Kaganoff's work is the first book on the subject (although there have been a number of articles). For those with an interest in the field, therefore, this book is virtually mandatory.

KOCH, H. W., *Medieval Warfare* (New York: Prentice-Hall, Inc., 1978). Another "coffee table" book, but replete with beautiful illustrations, many depicting excellent heraldry, and with extensive and fascinating text.

MACKINNON, CHARLES, *The Observer's Book of Heraldry* (London and New York: Frederick Warne and Company, 1966, 1972). This is one of a series of "Observer's" books. A pocket-sized volume, it is nevertheless well illustrated and informative. Its orientation is largely, if not entirely, British.

MANNING, ROSEMARY, *Heraldry* (London: A & C Black Limited, 1966, reprinted 1971). This is part of Black's Junior Reference Books series, and is written for younger readers. It, too, is largely British in scope.

MONCRIEFFE, IAIN, *Simple Heraldry* (Edinburgh: Thomas Nelson and Sons Limited, 1953; there have been several reprints). The author is the Scottish Kintyre Pursuivant of Arms; the illustrator, Don Pottinger, is "herald painter extraordinary to the Court of the Lord Lyon King of Arms." Only sixty-three pages, this book gives a quick, understandable, and good-humoredly illustrated summary of heraldry, especially as it exists in the British Isles.

NEUBECKER, OTTFRIED, *Heraldry: Sources, Symbols and Meaning* (New York: McGraw-Hill, 1976). This wide-ranging and lavishly illustrated work is written by the Director of the German General Roll of Arms, so for once, a fine reference work on heraldry is not overburdened with the arms of the British Isles. (There is, however, a considerable amount of information about German heraldry.) There is an extensive listing of collections of public heraldry in virtually every country where heraldry has existed, plus a fine bibliography on various national heraldries.

PINCHES, ROSEMARY, and ANTHONY WOOD, Eds., *A European Armorial* (London: Heraldry Today, 1971). Reproductions, in both color and

black and white, of several rolls of arms, offer the reader a veritable
cornucopia of charges. It also includes an introduction to Polish heraldry.

PINE, L. G., *International Heraldry* (Newton Abbot, Devon: David and
Charles, 1970). Although not a very extensive work, this book covers
many areas that others do not, such as the various provinces of Canada.

SCOTT-GILES, C. W., ed., *Motley Heraldry* (London: Tabard Publica-
tions; undated). This is probably a collector's item. Ostensibly written
by "the Fool of Arms," it is a slim volume of poetry dealing with various heraldic matters and events. No doubt the distinguished heraldist
(see below) had great fun in writing the book, as will anyone lucky
enough to read it. It is, incidentally, very thoroughly illustrated with
mostly legitimate coats of arms.

SCOTT-GILES, C. W., *The Romance of Heraldry* (London: J. M. Dent
and Sons Limited; New York: E. P. Dutton Company, Inc., 1967).
This book by the distinguished British Fitzalan Pursuivant of Arms Extraordinary was first published in 1929 and revised in subsequent publi-
cations. It has some excellent history, good black and white illustrations, and barely acknowledges heraldry in other countries except for
the "colonies" such as Canada and the United States.

SMITH, WHITNEY, *Flags: Through the Ages and Across the World* (New
York: McGraw-Hill, 1976). In size, style, and design this is a compan-
ion volume to Neubecker's *Heraldry: Sources, Symbols and Meaning*
(see above). The title essentially describes the content, but as vex-
illology (the study of flags) is intertwined with heraldry, this book contains much information and many illustrations dealing with the latter.
It is an excellent reference source for national emblems and for the use
of heraldry in designing flags.

TUCHMAN, BARBARA W., *A Distant Mirror: The Calamitous 14th Century* (New York: Alfred A. Knopf, Inc., 1978). This book, long on the
best-seller list, is a detailed and fascinating account of life in the Middle Ages and includes some engrossing information about the importance of heraldry in those days.

VERMONT, E. DE V., *America Heraldica* (New York: Heraldic Publishing
Company, 1965). Clearly, this is a facsimile of a book that was probably published toward the end of the nineteenth century. There is no
modern introduction to the book and there is no telling how authentic
the work is. On its title page it describes itself as: "A compilation of
coats of arms, crests and mottoes of prominent American families settled in this country before 1800." Its chief value, should you manage to
locate it in a library somewhere, is its illustrations and examples of
blazoning. Of course, there are coats of arms for a number of names,

each with charges you may want to adopt or adapt if your name is similar.

VON VOLBORTH, CARL ALEXANDER, *Heraldry of the World* (London: Blandford Press, 1973). This book is almost pocket-sized and it consists of only 250 pages. The author has nevertheless managed to cram into this estimable little volume a thorough introduction to heraldry and all its aspects, along with handsome color illustrations of the heraldry of most of the countries of Europe. The author is Danish, and there is a considerable amount of material on Scandinavian heraldry.

WEEKLEY, ERNEST, *The Romance of Names* (London: John Murray, 1914). A small, interesting, highly readable book that discusses in general how names originated and in particular several hundred English, Scottish, Welsh, and Irish surnames.

WESTIN, JEANE EDDY, *Finding Your Roots* (Los Angeles: J. P. Tarcher, Inc., 1977). In addition to offering a general introduction to genealogy, this book contains extensive information on how to conduct a genealogical search, along with many sources for information.

WHITE, T. H., *The Bestiary: A Book of Beasts* (New York: G. P. Putnam's Sons, 1954). If your public library does not own a copy of this book, it does not deserve to call itself a library. T. H. White took a bestiary that was written in the Middle Ages and translated it into modern English. Beautifully written, with a scholarly but nevertheless entertaining appendix discoursing on bestiaries, this work is a source book for every monster, real or imagined, known to twelfth-century man. It can serve beautifully for unusual and wholly acceptable heraldic charges.

Index